INSIDE CHINA'S SECRET PRISONS

INSIDE CHINA'S SECRET PRISONS

An Undercover Exposé and Its Lasting Legacy

ORVILLE SCHELL

Columbia University Press
New York

Columbia University Press
Publishers Since 1893
New York   Chichester, West Sussex
cup.columbia.edu

Cataloging-in-Publication Data is available from the Library of Congress.

ISBN 9780231221146 (hardback)
ISBN 9780231563574 (epub)
ISBN 9780231565813 (PDF)

LCCN 2026022897

Printed in the United States of America

Cover design: Milenda Nan Ok Lee
Cover art: gopixa / Shutterstock

GPSR Authorized Representative: Easy Access System Europe, Mustamäe tee 50, 10621 Tallinn, Estonia, gpsr.requests@easproject.com

To my three sons, Orville Hickok Schell IV, Jonathan Sebastian Schell, and Alexander Shawn Schell, and to my dear wife Baifang Schell.

For giving me a family and meaning to my life.

Just because things have always been this way, does that then make it right?

从来如此，便对么？

—Lu Xun 鲁迅, “Diary of a Madman” (狂人日记), 1918

CONTENTS

Part I

REPRISING SOMETHING PAST

Chapter One

AN EXCAVATION

IN 2021, just after the death of my wife, Baifang, I was looking through some boxes of old papers when I chanced upon a yellowing manuscript. As I began leafing through it, I immediately recognized it as the long-form piece I had written for *The New Yorker*, for which I was China correspondent from 1975 into the mid-1990s. The manuscript chronicled a project I had worked on for nearly a year with an investigative team from the CBS News program *60 Minutes*. Our assignment had been to document the prison camp system that arced across the People's Republic of China (PRC), held many political prisoners, and was reported to be illegally exporting goods made in prison factories with forced labor into the United States.

Uncovering this relic from three decades ago made me feel a little like an archaeologist stumbling onto an ancient text hidden in a long-sealed tomb. The article was drawn from a journal I had kept throughout the nine-month *60 Minutes* investigation into China's vast "reform-through-labor camp, or *laogai*, system" (劳改体制) that was aired by CBS in the fall of 1991.

After the broadcast, I had set to work writing a narrative piece for *The New Yorker* about this dangerous and exciting but often hair-raising investigation. However, it was not until after the magazine had edited my draft that I fully came to my senses and realized that identifying myself so closely with this cloak-and-dagger investigation and drawing back the veil on China's prison and forced labor systems would provoke the wrath of the Chinese Communist Party (CCP). Fearful of the consequences not only for my own career as a China writer but also for the future of my Chinese-born wife, her Beijing-based parents, and our many friends still living in China, I decided, after much agonizing, to withdraw the piece from publication.

When I first rediscovered this lost-and-found manuscript, I expected to quickly conclude that after three decades, its shelf life would have long since expired. However, as I began leafing through its pages, several things surprised me. First, the saga still made for a really exciting story. Second, because a new global debate over yet another generation of goods made with forced labor had erupted in the United States, the issue of prison labor was more relevant than ever. This was especially true of goods made in China's westernmost province, Xinjiang, which had a land mass four times the size of California and was home to an estimated twelve million Uyghur Muslims. Now thousands of them were reported to be under detention in a newly built network of high-tech prison camps, many of which had attached production facilities. These new camps had engendered a whole a new wave of antagonism over the still divisive issue of prison labor and was once again bedeviling U.S.-China relations.

When, in 2012–13, Xi Jinping became enthroned as Chinese president and then Party general secretary, the era of "reform and opening" (改革开放) initiated by Deng Xiaoping in 1978 largely came to an end. Despite grave setbacks, like the Beijing Massacre in 1989, when thousands of peaceful protesters were killed and wounded by People's Liberation Army (PLA) soldiers around Tiananmen Square, by the 2000s China's reform era had lasted for two and a half decades. This interregnum had allowed Chinese and foreigners alike to hope that the PRC's Maoist system might slowly become more open and rules-based. And for a while it seemed possible to many observers that this "people's republic" might actually be able to slowly morph out of its revolutionary chrysalis and adopt a more democratic, humane form of governance.

However, early in his tenure Xi seemed to have concluded that only a system of strict Leninist political controls could ever hold Chinese society together. After more than the two decades of reform that had allowed not only for greater openness but also for an impressive recrudescence of "wealth and power" (富强), Xi began reversing China's gears. Because he chronically feared that "hostile foreign forces" (敌对势力) were at work undermining his vaunted "socialism with Chinese characteristics" (中国特色社会主义), he began centralizing power and even decoupling key supply chains from the United States and other democratic countries, the very partners that had helped champion Deng's reforms and make China prosperous. In important ways, Xi seemed to be politically returning his country to the very past that so many of his fellow leaders had spent so much effort trying to vacate. Xi's new political glide path of once again "putting the party first" (把党放在首位) left many longtime China observers like me surprised and even bewildered.

The challenge our *60 Minutes* project confronted three decades ago was a herculean one: how to document China's vast gulag of prisons and penal enterprises that were surreptitiously exporting into the global marketplace. As the project gathered momentum, it became a joint-venture chapter in the lives of both my wife and me that we would never forget.

This epic saga began early in the winter of 1991 when a producer at the weekly CBS television investigative news program *60 Minutes* approached me about helping with a project focusing on political imprisonment in China. Although by then I had been covering China for nearly three decades as a writer, I knew few details about its extensive penal system. However, I did understand that probing these dark and sensitive interstices of the Chinese Communist Revolution would pose substantial risks to us all. For the CCP was notoriously allergic to anyone who defied it by exposing any of its manifold contradictions. A friend of ours, one of China's foremost independent thinkers and a former political prisoner, Dai Qing, described the Party's response to those who defied and embarrassed it in her book *My Imprisonment* (我的入狱) this way: "I realize now that the thing that infuriates them most of all is insubordination. They don't mind what else you do: embezzle money, plagiarize, or whatever. All else can be forgiven; but to be disobedient is completely unacceptable." Doing a *60 Minutes* program on China's reform-through-labor camp system on American TV would certainly be considered the highest kind of insubordination by the Party.

Because Baifang had had far more experience with China's repressive political system than I, she was very skeptical about taking on this project. Making matters even more complicated, we had just learned that she was pregnant and were fearful of getting sucked into a political whirlpool that would be harmful to our unborn baby. After all, *60 Minutes* was seeking to penetrate one of the most sensitive parts of Chinese life, an enormous penal colony that the Party had made every effort to keep hidden from public scrutiny.

Needless to say, rediscovering my manuscript, especially just after Baifang's death, triggered a whole flood of painful memories and emotions. As I reread what I had written, I could not help but remember how, despite her reservations, she had ended up being extremely loyal and supportive.

Another thing that struck me about what I had written was how, after so many revolutions, reforms, rejuvenations, counterrevolutions, and even a crypto-capitalist economic boom, China in the 2020s was still wrestling with many of the same institutional problems that had drawn our attention three decades before. One of those enduring problems was its tradition of political imprisonment, forced labor, and the maintenance of a vast penal system on which the Party depended as a control mechanism against political dissent. Despite all the changes China had undergone in the intervening years, the Party still tenaciously defended arbitrary detention, continued to incarcerate large populations of political prisoners, and still subjected many of them to forced labor. And now the global media were once again awash with reports and stories focusing on China's new generation of prisons and forced labor. This time the lens was focused on the tens of thousands of Uyghur Muslims in Xinjiang Province who were being detained in a new generation of detention facilities where many were still compelled to do forced labor.

These new camps were justified by Beijing as part of an anti-terrorist campaign against Muslim separatism that had triggered Xi Jinping into ramping up a whole new campaign of extra-judicial incarceration, political imprisonment, and forced labor practices. In fact, Beijing had ordered managers at prison factories, mines, and farms in Xinjiang to update backward production facilities, install new equipment, implement more streamlined business practices, and continue to illegally export prison-made goods into unwary global markets. The last thing Xi Jinping welcomed was the prying eyes of foreign correspondents, civil society activists, probing academic researchers, and data hungry foreign consultants undertaking due diligence on local companies and state-owned enterprises, especially if such research was done from Chinese soil, as our *60 Minutes* project had been done.

Now, here in my hands, was the written record of that underground investigation, carried out right under the nose of the Chinese government and then broadcast on American commercial network television. So great was the Party's embarrassment and so great was my fear about its retaliation that I had withdrawn the manuscript from publication.

Under Xi Jinping I knew that retaliation would be even more extreme than under Jiang Zemin. China was now far richer, more powerful, and more inclined to respond punitively to criticisms or exposés. And I was still deeply connected to China. My family still had an apartment in Beijing, where my parents-in-law continued to live. Also, I still had friends there, although absence had made many of those relationships fade. So, as I contemplated the prospect of belatedly publishing this still radioactive manuscript, familiar fears of excommunication that had been such an important form of pressure during my earlier life came rushing back in.

However, as I continued pondering what to do now, I was surprised to find my reaction slowly changing. First, the idea of returning to China without Baifang began to feel almost indecent. Indeed, it was hard to even imagine being there without her. And the longer I pondered the notion of not returning, the more willing I found myself to accept the idea. Paradoxically, I even began to feel an unexpected sensation of relief. In a way I had previously never fully considered, I began to see more clearly than ever just how debilitating it had been to live in a constant state of anxiety over being shut out of this country on which so much of my professional life depended.

Perhaps I should not have been surprised by this reaction. After all, I was now in my eighties and no longer in need of returning to China to make or maintain my professional career or place in the universe. So, instead of feeling anxiety about the thought of never returning, I began to feel a sense of welcome calm. If I did not *want* to return, the Party no longer had a lever of control over me, over what I could write, say, and do.

I could do whatever I wished. I had to admit that the sense of emancipation that overcame me was truly intoxicating.

I have consciously chosen the word *emancipation*, not *liberation*, because the latter term has been so abused by the Party in China that I can no longer bear to let it pass my lips. Propagandists have spoken unendingly of "before the liberation (解放) of the Chinese people in 1949," "the Peoples Liberation Army," "the liberation of Tibet," "the War of Liberation against the Nationalists," and the like, while in reality throughout this high-tide period of the Chinese Communist Revolution, the Chinese people were becoming quasi-prisoners. While the term *liberation* may still have respectability in other societies and circumstances, in China it has been so corrupted as to be rendered unusable . . . except by true believers, propagandists, or critics who deploy it in the most sarcastic, ironic of ways.

Two American Fulbright scholars who were imprisoned and "brainwashed" in the early 1950s in China as Mao came to power wrote a book about their travails entitled *Prisoners of Liberation*. Although I am not sure it was their intention, this wonderfully ironic title perfectly captured the paradox of the Chinese Communist Revolution: Through misuse, so many terms and words had come to mean their opposite.

One of the things that drew me back to China on the hundreds of trips I have made since 1975 was the excitement of watching the country and society metamorphose from Maoism to . . . well, that was hard to say. During the late 1970s and 1980s it was often very difficult to know just where China was headed. But to watch this spellbinding but always uncertain drama unfold was like having a front row seat at a great performance.

China had changed so much since I began following it in the early 1960s that the promise of more to come, especially during the 1980s and '90s, filled many of us watching with a certain curiosity and excitement, if not optimism. However, by the time Xi Jinping arrived, there began to be a clash of dreams at work. Whereas Xi's dream was of a "rejuvenated" China using its new wealth and power to streamline its autocracy and enhance its global status so that it could reorder the world to serve his own hegemonic interests, the dream of people like me was different. We dreamed of a China that was not just wealthy and more powerful but dedicated to fusing its traditions of eastern Confucian and Buddhist humanism together with western Enlightenment thinking to generate a society and country that was more modern, intelligent, open, tolerant, and not always so at odds with the outside world as it had been during the Mao era. Because I was able to share—and to some extent even live—this dream with my wife, what might otherwise have been a solitary, largely vicarious scholarly/journalistic enterprise became a far more personal experience.

The rediscovery of my manuscript in the middle of the Xi era made me wonder whether I had done the right thing three decades before when, concerned about provoking the CCP, I had withdrawn it from publication. What I had done back then, during a far more relaxed period under Jiang Zemin, begged the question: Had efforts to propitiate, or at least not provoke, the CCP ever benefited U.S.-China relations, or anyone except the Party?

In my own experience, whenever I, or someone else, made a concession in the spirit of goodwill, the Party simply pocketed it without reciprocation and then, all too often, demanded even more concessions. So, if I threw this manuscript back into its box and forgot about it a second time, I doubted there would be any more reciprocation or recompense this time than thirty years ago.

As his term without limits as supreme leader continued, Xi seemed to agree with his father's mantra: "The Party's interest comes first" (党的利在首位). He also seemed to view the United States—a "hostile foreign force"—as an increasingly implacable adversary that the CCP had to do everything it could to defend itself against. Under these circumstances, it was hardly surprising that Americans also began adopting an increasingly negative view of China. Gallup polls showed U.S. favorability ratings for China dropping steadily, from 72 percent in early 1989 to only 14 percent in 2023. Those numbers continued to fall as more and more Americans asked themselves: "What's the point of continuing to propitiate China if Xi's conception of 'win-win' means China wins twice?"

I had spent decades organizing academic, political, and cultural exchanges in an effort to "build bridges" across the U.S.-China divide. However, because my parallel work was as a writer, I was still relegated to the "unfriendly" rather than the "friendly" category by the Party. Indeed, it was very difficult to be an honest writer about China, because covering it often involved being critical, and being critical inevitably engendered access problems. So, as I reedited this manuscript for a second try at publishing, I understood that exposing my involvement in the *60 Minutes* project now would, even several decades later, still have dire consequences.

Thirty years ago, I had considered following former Czech President Vaclav Havel's admonition to "speak truth to power," publish this piece in *The New Yorker* as planned, and let the devil take the hindmost. However, in the end, the downside risk loomed so large that I yielded. Now, however, the situation had changed. My life's partner was gone, so I no longer needed to worry about her welfare. Her parents still lived in Beijing, but they were so elderly the Party did not care about them. Being older myself, I no longer needed to be so concerned about having my own career damaged. And since my children were now grown, I did not need to be so mindful of maintaining a connection to their mother's birthplace for them. So, even if it meant banishment forever, I decided to go ahead.

Chapter Two

FALLING UNDER CHINA'S THRALL

MY PATHWAY TO CHINA was a circuitous one. I came of age in a New York City family where world affairs were regular dinnertime grist for discussions. My mother had a natural interest in global issues. She had opposed atmospheric nuclear testing in the 1950s, supported the civil rights movement in the 1960s, and protested the Vietnam War in the 1970s. While my father was a corporate lawyer, he was deeply drawn to the ideals of international justice and human rights. Along with Random House president Robert Bernstein, he became one of the founders of Human Rights Watch. He also became the president of the Bar Association of the City of New York, where in his always understated but principled way he led young lawyers to Washington, D.C. to speak out against rights abuses both at home and abroad. So, in profound ways our parents influenced the intellectual and political trajectories not only of me but also of my older sister, Suzanne, and younger brother, Jonathan, who also became a writer at *The New Yorker.*

Curiously, my father was almost born in China. After graduating from Yale University in 1900 and then from Johns Hopkins Medical School in 1906, my grandfather, whose name both my father and I shared, departed for China with my grandmother. Their mission was to help establish the first Western medical school in China, which came to be known as the Hsiang-Ya Medical College or the Changsha-Yale Medical College, founded by Yale University near Mao Zedong's hometown in China's inland province of Hunan. To get to Changsha, my grandparents had to make the arduous trip up raging rapids in the Yangtze River via a junk pulled by Chinese "trackers" (纤夫).

While in China, my grandmother became pregnant. She became so overcome by morning sickness that they had to return to Shanghai and then New Rochelle, New York, for the birth of my father in 1908. And so, I grew up in a home where Chinese curiosities were around the house, inoculating me with an acquaintance of things from that distant and then still exotic land.

However, it was not until my undergraduate years at Harvard in the 1960s that by happenstance I became initiated into Chinese studies.

My sister, Suzanne, and I wanted to take a class together before she graduated two years ahead of me, and we could only find one that matched both our schedules, the legendary survey course on East Asia, officially listed in the Harvard course catalog as Social Sciences 111 but fondly known among students as "rice paddies." It was taught by John King Fairbank, the grand progenitor of American China studies; Edwin Reischauer, future U.S. ambassador to Japan; Benjamin Schwartz, a brilliant intellectual historian; and sundry other Harvard faculty members.

To help undergraduates penetrate China's elusiveness, each student was issued a weighty mimeographed text on China, Japan, and Korea that Fairbank and Reischauer were just then finishing as a two-volume book set. This tome came accessorized with a foldout, color-coded "Chronological Chart of Far Eastern History" that showed all the Chinese, Japanese, and Korean imperial dynasties that had risen and fallen during the previous three millennia. Our professors doubtless hoped that this visual aid would give us neophyte scholars a graphic sense of the sweep of China's succession of rising and falling dynasties by dividing them into neatly color-coded historical segments. To my untutored eyes, however, this chart made dynastic history only look long, repetitious, and impenetrable.

Nonetheless, I became intrigued by China, especially by Mao Zedong's strange combination of revolutionary bravado and aloofness from the world. Perhaps the most cryptically seductive aspect of China's revolution was that, as an American, I was unable to go there. For when PLA troops ended up in combat with American GIs during the Korea War in the early 1950s, the Cold War became so cold that travel for Americans to the People's Republic of China became forbidden. The closest we could get to the epicenter of Mao's revolution was Taiwan and the British Crown colony of Hong Kong, where we could at least meet Chinese refugees, read Chinese

Communist newspapers, watch films from Shanghai, buy books from Beijing, and dream of crossing the border someday ourselves. Far from repelling me, China's closed door only beckoned. Any place that kept itself so cloistered, I surmised, must be hiding some very interesting secrets.

In 1961, after floundering through a summer of Chinese language at Stanford University, instead of returning to Harvard, I set out for Asia to continue studying Chinese on Taiwan. But, because I had an errant uncle living in Tahiti, I decided to first ship out for Papeete as a third cook aboard an aging Norwegian freighter, the *Thorsisle*, and try to island-hop across the Pacific Ocean to Taiwan. My parents back in New York City feared I would follow in my uncle's footsteps, become a Gauguin-like beachcomber in Tahiti, hook up with a local vahine, stay on in Polynesia, and forsake my Harvard education.

However, instead of jumping ship in Tahiti, I stayed with the *Thorisle*, went on to Samoa, Fiji, New Caledonia, and New Guinea and finally did land up on Taiwan, where I procured a modest fellowship (paid in cash each month!) at National Taiwan University. While there, I even had the opportunity on several occasions to meet Chiang Kai-shek, who had fled the Chinese mainland for the island after losing the Chinese Civil War to Mao in 1949. The generalissimo—the G-Mo, as he was known—was a larger-than-life leader whom the world was then ignominiously passing by. There was a wistfulness hanging over my meetings with him—arranged by the Chinese Counter Attack the Mainland and Rescue Our Fellow Countrymen Youth League (中国青年反共救国团)!—which only made me yearn all the more to get to Beijing, where Chairman

Mao presided and appeared to be "making revolution" (搞革命) on a monumental scale.

I finally got to Beijing early in 1975 as part of another "youth work delegation" (青年劳动代表团) approved by Premier Zhou Enlai to keep a few doors open to the United States and organized by the Chinese People's Association for Friendship with Foreign Countries (中国人民对外友好协会). As we crossed the border from Hong Kong, I was so filled with excitement at the prospect of spending the next few months working in the People's Republic of China—first on the Dazhai Model Agricultural Brigade and then in the Shanghai Electrical Machinery Factory—I could hardly contain myself.

However, my time inside China proved deeply confusing. Because I had already spent almost two years living in Taiwan, where I had even had a girlfriend who spoke no English, I thought I had become acquainted with the basic skills of navigating Chinese life. In Mao's "New China," however, I felt completely lost. I ended up feeling as if I had been dropped into a theme park where nothing was real. As it turned out, much of what we saw was not real and, for understandable reasons, people were simply too afraid to interact spontaneously with us as Americans.

Experiencing the closed nature of Mao's "socialist society" firsthand was a wake-up call that helped catalyze my own interest in openness, freedom, liberty, and human rights as critical elements in any healthy society. I had caught a firsthand glimpse of how China's party strictures deformed human life in China. But I must confess that, at the time, I was not sure how to read what I had just experienced. For this state of affairs seemed just to be the way China was, and would stay.

And yet, when Mao died in 1976, Deng Xiaoping, unexpectedly returning from political oblivion, initiated a pragmatic agenda of "reform and opening" (改革开放) and catalyzed a surprising new efflorescence of change, openness, and optimism in society. As these reforms gathered momentum, many of us onlookers were tempted to imagine that China might yet vacate some of its most oppressive internal policies and even find new ways to engage with democratic capitalist countries like the United States. Such hopes were soon reinforced for me in a most personal way: I fell in love with and married Liu Baifang, who gave what was happening in China a new and very personal dimension.

Our creation myth began in 1986 when I reluctantly agreed to host a group of PRC scholars from UC Berkeley's Center for Chinese Studies, where I had started my own graduate work, for a visit to the cattle ranch I was then operating with a partner on the Pacific coast north of San Francisco. As the delegation arrived, I was startled when a young Chinese woman emerged from the van behind a string of men. Liu Baifang moved with such understated grace and smiled with such radiance it was difficult for me not to stare. As I showed the visitors around our corrals, hay barn, and feedlot filled with our herd of mooing Angus/Hereford cross beef cattle, I felt her presence like a laser beam. Before the delegation departed, I somehow managed to inveigle her phone number.

The next day when I called, she accepted my invitation to dinner in San Francisco and a one-man theatrical production by an actor friend of mine who was playing a deranged fundamentalist preacher, Reverend Billy. I wasn't sure what she made of me or the performance, but I was smitten.

We began going out, and then she became my wife. And so, just as China was becoming one of the most exciting stories in the world, we began our almost four-decades-long odyssey together. But even during those heady days of audacious reform and high-speed social, cultural, economic, and even political change, the PRC remained a one-party state, its expansive gulag endured, and forced labor continued to be used in its prison enterprises. In fact, in the crackdown that followed the 1989 Tiananmen Square demonstrations for greater democracy and then the Beijing Massacre on June 4th, far from withering away, China's enormous, multilayered prison system underwent a period of restoration and growth. As Chinese prisons filled with a new generation of political dissidents, it became understandable how sinologists might have earlier viewed China as having a tendency to endlessly circle back on itself. Despite all the monumental reforms and changes the 1980s brought, the basic structure of the political system Mao had borrowed from Stalin and the Soviet Union in the 1950s not only remained intact but was again becoming a bulwark against yet another generation of political opposition.

Part II

HOW IT ALL BEGAN

Chapter Three

AN UNLIKELY IDEA

ONE FEBRUARY MORNING in 1991 as I arrived at New York's Empire State Building to attend a Human Rights Watch board meeting, I was handed a message. Someone named David Gelber at CBS News wanted to talk with me.

It turned out that Gelber was with *60 Minutes*, the well-known CBS newsmagazine program famous for featuring hard-hitting investigative reports from around the world. Hosted by anchor/correspondents such as Mike Wallace, Morley Safer, Lesley Stahl, Dan Rather, Diane Sawyer, and Ed Bradley, and produced by Don Hewitt, *60 Minutes* was perhaps the most respected investigative program on commercial American television. And since it aired Sunday evenings just after the CBS network's popular National Football League broadcasts, it had an enormous viewership.

When I called Gelber, he told me he produced segments for anchor Ed Bradley and they were interested in doing something on political imprisonment in China. Although I was well aware of how difficult it would be to pull back the veil on China's huge but secretive array of penal colonies, I was nonetheless curious to learn more about what Gelber had in mind. Such investigations inside China had become all the more difficult because of the crackdown after the 1989 Beijing Massacre as large numbers of new dissidents were imprisoned for political reasons and the very negative global response made Chinese leaders more suspicious than ever of foreign media activities.

The more Gelber tried to explain his thinking, the more naive he sounded. How did he ever expect to get CBS crews into China to report on a topic as sensitive as political imprisonment, much less gain access to China's extensive network (劳改营)?

"I appreciate your impulse," I told him, trying not to sound too dismissive. "But I don't think it's doable."

"OK," he countered. "But let's atleast have lunch and talk."

The following day, we met at a midtown restaurant.

Gelber was a smart New Yorker with the kind of high-voltage intensity characteristic of many network TV producers. But he also had a sweetness of manner that shone through when he smiled. Although he clearly was an astute person, his limited knowledge of China made him credulous about how things actually worked and what foreign journalists might actually expect to be able to accomplish there.

"Hey, would it be possible to find that guy who stopped those tanks in Tiananmen Square in 1989?" he suddenly asked, with disarming innocence. "Could we do something with him?"

"The 'Tankman'?" I snorted.

"Yeah."

The Tankman, as he had come to be known, was the young man who, carrying several shopping bags, had appeared during the massacre in 1989 on the Avenue of Eternal Peace near Tiananmen Square to step in front of an advancing column of PLA tanks. A videographer in the nearby Peking Hotel had recorded him stopping them in their tracks, and the images had ricocheted around the world to become the symbol of resistance against the Chinese government. But, as quickly as the Tankman himself appeared on global television screens, he disappeared.

"No one in the outside world ever learned who he was, much less what happened to him," I told Gelber.

"Well," he persisted, "could we get into some Chinese prisons instead, and . . . ?"

"It's a police state," I reminded him. "At most we might get into a model prison or two. But officials wouldn't let us near one of their real facilities, especially if its prison ran factories using forced labor to manufacture goods for export."

"So, how would you do this story?" he asked, throwing the challenge back to me.

I frankly did not have an answer, because to me his idea seemed fanciful at best. I told him about a Chinese journalist I had met, Jia Lusheng, who was part of the "investigative literature" (报告文学) movement in the 1980s and had actually infiltrated several "reform-through-labor" camps in Xinjiang Province by donning ragged clothing and moving along what he called the "dark path" (黑道) among China's "floating population" (流动人口) of beggars, itinerant workers, drifters, and dispossessed people. During that decade, such rural immigrants had flooded Chinese cities as low-cost laborers who ended up driving much of the early industrialization and the privatization of the economy. Jia had even written a book in Chinese about his exploits, *The Great Prisons of Western China* (中国西部大监狱), that provided a tantalizing glimpse of what it was like to be caught in this remote world of incarceration.

I also mentioned a young Frenchman, Marc Boulet, who had married a woman from Beijing and not only spoke good Chinese, but his dark hair and complexion make him look like a Uyghur Muslim. He had also managed to penetrate some prison camps in Xinjiang, and had written a book, *Dans la Peau d'un Chinois*, about his secretive exploits.

Then there was the well-known Chinese writer Zhang Xianliang (张贤亮), who had been detained during the Anti-Rightist Campaign for writing "counterrevolutionary" poetry and spent twenty-two years "sitting in prison" (坐牢). In the early 1990s, he published a journal-based novel, *Grass Soup* (烦恼就是智慧) and several works of fiction, including *Getting Used to Dying* (习惯死亡) and *Half of Man Is Woman* (男人的一半是女人), that documented his time in the camps. As Zhang had wryly observed of China's twisted reform-through-labor system, here was "a Communist country that had incarcerated as enemies of Communism people, who in fact, yearned for a true Communist system."

"Getting someone like that on board would be great!" Gelber enthusiastically offered. "But, remember, we're doing TV, so we can't just have writers. We have to get into some real prisons with cameras."

"Well, good luck with that," I responded, rolling my eyes. "Anyway, most of the people I just mentioned worked during the freewheeling 1980s. But now, after the 1989 Beijing Massacre, things are very different."

Gelber looked disappointed.

I left lunch feeling that *60 Minutes* was on a wild-goose chase. In the two years since the Beijing Massacre, controls had become so tight, it was virtually impossible for anyone, especially foreigners, to engage in the kinds independent research or investigative activities that had formerly been possible. Nonetheless, despite my pessimism, I promised Gelber I would keep thinking about the challenge. Over the days that followed, I was unable to completely put his invitation aside. After all, how often did one get presented with an opportunity to carry out such an interesting and important investigative project with all the necessary resources provided?

■ ■ ■

As I continued mulling over Gelber's challenge, I could not see how such an investigation could be successfully undertaken, especially by a program like *60 Minutes* that demanded never-before-seen footage, drama, sleuthing, "door-stepping" of unwary suspects, and confrontational interviews. Overcoming such challenges in China made the prospect of success exceedingly small. What is more, how would outsiders ever get bulky video equipment secretly inside prison camps? Even the planning of such a venture would be risky. Not only was China an authoritarian state, but despite the enormity and vastness of its penal archipelago, facilities were well guarded. To even begin documenting the variety of raw materials, agricultural products, and manufactured goods this sprawling system of prison enterprises produced would require a Chinese investigator who was knowledgeable, bold, courageous, and savvy enough to know how to operate and, should trouble arise, how to drop out of sight.

If such a person did magically appear, the challenges would still be formidable. Even in Deng's pre-1989 China, where a far more open society afforded much wider social margins uncontrolled by the government, undertaking such an investigation would have been difficult. In post-1989 China, where unmonitored space had shrunk, eluding the state had become all but impossible. And so, the more I pondered Gelber's idea, the more dubious I became.

Besides, what kind of a useful role could I play? More importantly, did I even want a role? As a foreigner unable to disguise myself, any in-country involvement would be extremely dangerous. No matter how good one's Chinese language skills were or what connections one had, Westerners in China were still viewed indelibly as outsiders. It was no accident that the Chinese term for "foreigner" was literally "people from an outside country" (外国人).

■ ■ ■

Nonetheless, wanting to learn more about China's reform-through-labor system (劳动改造制度), or *laogai* system, I visited the Center for Chinese Studies library at the University of California, Berkeley. There I found some relevant books, including several autobiographical accounts by Americans and Europeans who had been incarcerated on vague charges of espionage when Mao came to power in 1949 and a few on Chinese who had been detained extrajudicially on nebulous political charges such as being "rightists" (右派), "counterrevolutionaries" (反革命分子) or in one of the other "five black categories" (黑五类).

China's prison camp system was made up of a bewildering archipelago of penal facilities at almost every level of government in every part of the country. They included ordinary jails (监狱), administrative detention centers (治安行政拘留所), judicial detention centers (司法拘留所), general detention centers (看守所), Central Commission for Discipline and Inspection detention centers (中央纪委部留置场所), "reform-through-labor detachments" (劳动改造队), and "reeducation-through-labor detachments" (劳动教养队) [technically abolished in 2013], to name only some of the major categories of prisons that the Party maintained for people it viewed as social and political malefactors.

In the reform-through-labor universe, there was one last murky category known as "forced job placement" (留场就业), a term used for inmates who had finished their formal reform-through-labor sentences but no longer had homes to return to because they had been imprisoned for so long, their families and friends had renounced them, forgotten them, or died.

With no place to go, these inmates were allowed to continue working in their old prison camp enterprises as poorly paid laborers, but to live on the outside.

Although China's *laogai* system had been borrowed from Stalin, it also had its own "Chinese characteristics" (中国特色) that distinguished it from its Soviet counterpart. One element that made it unique was the way it combined punishment with both "thought reform" (思想改造) and "labor reform" (劳动改造).

A Beijing University publication I found at UC Berkeley explained the logic of combining forced labor with thought reform: "Except for those who must be exterminated physically due to political considerations, human beings must be utilized as a productive force with submissiveness as a prerequisite." It went on to note that "the fundamental policy is: Forced labor is the means, while thought reform is the basic aim." Here, one cannot help but think of the signs that hung on the gates of Auschwitz, Sachsenhausen, Dachau, and other German death camps proclaiming "*Arbeit macht frei*" ("Work makes one free").

In other words, forced labor and thought reform—more commonly referred to in the United States as "brainwashing" (洗脑)—formed a kind of *yin* (阴) and *yang* (阳) relationship with each other. They were complementary processes designed to collectively purge a prisoner—whether a criminal or political prisoner—of whatever wrong behavior or "incorrect political thinking" (错误思想). they were seen as being afflicted by. The practice of brainwashing was perfected early in Mao's revolution as a companion therapy for political miscreants who stubbornly resisted the tonic effects of imprisonment and forced labor and therefore required an even deeper "rectification of thought" (思想整顿).

A *Criminal Reform Handbook* issued by the Ministry of Justice in 1988 explained the rationale for forced labor this way: "The [prison] system organizes criminals in labor and production, thus creating wealth for society." Then, it noted that by "representing the working class and the working people of our country," China's reform-through-labor system "exercises dictatorship over a minority of elements who are hostile to socialism, thus safeguard[ing] our socialist system."

The reform-through-labor system underwent some reassessment in the early 1980s, when leaders like Xi Jinping's own father, Xi Zhongxun, a revolutionary veteran, was brought out of political exile to help revive the National People's Congress in the wake of the Cultural Revolution. In 1981, Xi Zhongxun was put in charge of the Congress's Legislative Committee, where one of his assignments was to look at the institutions of China's reform-through-labor system, the very system in which he himself had been imprisoned.

Xi's take was somewhat surprising. He concluded that while *laogai* inmates might have done some wrong things, many were also victims of what he called "leftover poisons" from the Anti-Rightist Campaign, the Great Leap Forward, and the Cultural Revolution, when those in charge of the camps had prioritized force and abusive tactics over the rights of inmates. A subsequent Ministry of Public Security conference on the *laogai* system called for a new policy that would include a modicum of "revolutionary humanism," even going so far as to speak of the need for leaders to run camps more "like parents treating a sick child rather than disciplining unruly students."

While Xi abjured from totally rejecting the notion of reform through labor, in one speech he observed: "After prisoners are sentenced and they are laboring at a *laogai* facility, if you do not treat them as people, if you abuse and humiliate them, or even engage in a fascist dictatorship, wouldn't that also be the influence of leftism?" "Leftism" and "rightism" were two erroneous, if nebulous, tendencies that kept manifesting themselves in Party history, causing many to be grievously punished.

Implementing a rule of law did make some halting progress in China during the 1980s. However, the *laogai* system continued unchecked. Moreover, many of the reforms that were implemented were set back by the political crackdown that followed the Beijing Massacre in 1989. The ensuing retrenchment not only served as the death knell for more meaningful political reforms but gave hard-line conservative veterans in the Party cause to insist that the *laogai* system still had utility and should remain.

Chapter Four

A GREEN LIGHT

WHEN I SPOKE to Gelber on the phone from California and asked how the project was progressing back at *60 Minutes* headquarters in New York City, he hesitantly responded, "Well, we'll have to see what happens."

While waiting for a dictum, trade volumes between the United States and China had only increased. In fact, by 1991, the United States had become the PRC's largest foreign investor, with some 1,200 American companies already investing a total of $4.2 billion, a figure that was expected to continue climbing. All this burgeoning trade and investment had made American CEOs more inclined to keep urging Washington to disregard political differences with Beijing, even to overlook things like rights abuses, intellectual property theft, forced labor, and Chinese dumping in U.S. markets. China was a vast market, and there was money to be made!

However, because there was still general opposition to the PRC's political system, a vigorous debate raged in the U.S. Congress over whether to regrant China MFN (most favored nation) trade status that conferred the lowest tariffs on Chinese exports to the United States. A growing number of U.S. political leaders were blaming the escalating trade imbalance on unfair Chinese trade practices and protectionist policies. In fact, U.S. Trade Representative Carla Hills had just listed China as a "trade-restricting nation," a designation that required the United States to formally consider taking retaliatory measures.

So, despite the reluctance of many U.S. companies to openly criticize Beijing's policies, a combination of Chinese protectionism, unfair and illegal trading practices, theft of intellectual property, forced-labor issues, and growing trade imbalances had made many members of Congress reluctant to regrant China MFN trade status, as President George H. W. Bush had done the year before and now sought to do again.

As Gelber waited for a dictum from higher-ups at *60 Minutes*, I was becoming more and more uncertain about getting involved. Their idea seemed both vague and almost impossible to pull off. My only direct experience with Chinese prisons had been two visits to "model" penal facilities years before, the first in Shanghai in 1975, and the second in Shenyang in 1979, where some of the prisoners had been incarcerated for crimes of "counterrevolution" (反革命) and other political offenses. Fully cognizant that any unscripted comments, especially to visiting foreigners, would get them into serious trouble, when called on to speak, these "model prisoners" robotically acknowledged that their punishments were fully justified and praised the Party's magnanimity for giving them a second chance to cleanse themselves of whatever "crimes" had landed them in prison. But their pale faces, shaved heads, and unresponsive manners said far more than their verbal responses to our earnest questions.

One thing had always perplexed me about China's prison and forced labor systems: Why, as the country opened up to the outside world and was so successfully developing and modernizing, did the Party continue to cling so tenaciously to such a retrograde and embarrassing set of penal institutions that, when exposed abroad, only gave China black eyes? Why did leaders in Beijing keep subjecting themselves to such predictable global disapprobation? Even more perplexing, why, when products made by these prison enterprises were discovered by U.S. customs agents, were officials instructed to be so strident in defending the indefensible?

As a study prepared by the Library of Congress for the Senate Foreign Relations Committee reported, a 1988 provincial Chinese publication, *Yearbook of Local Historical Records for Shandong*, blatantly acknowledged that reform-through-labor camp enterprises in the province had for more than thirty years been exporting goods and commodities to eighty-one foreign countries and regions on five continents "in exchange for large amounts of foreign currency." Such statements in official publications made official denials sound even more specious.

■ ■ ■

When Gelber and I spoke again, he had still not heard back from *60 Minutes* executive producer Don Hewitt. As in

Hollywood, where film executives express boundless enthusiasm for ideas that never get into production, this project seemed to be suffering a similar fate: death by enthusiasm. Although I did not say this to Gelber, I, too, was beginning to think maybe it would be just as well if the idea quietly passed into oblivion. With Baifang pregnant, I was more and more dubious about getting involved in such a dangerous and uncertain undertaking. That said, as more verdicts and sentences against political dissidents kept being announced, my sense of the seriousness of the subject only grew. If *60 Minutes* did finally want to proceed, would it not be a kind of moral dereliction of duty to drop out just because of worries about my family and my own future?

Each new political arrest was a reminder of just how much influence the Mao era still exerted on China's present. For example, when the twenty-eighth anniversary of his campaign to "Learn from Comrade Lei Feng" arrived in March, the media exploded with encomiums to this model hero from the People's Liberation Army who had been the centerpiece of a mass propaganda campaign launched by Mao himself in 1963 to venerate "proletarian heroes" (无产阶级英雄). It was Lei who had made such unctuous declarations of Party loyalty as "Whatever Chairman Mao says, I will do" and "I have only one desire in my heart: I want to be wholeheartedly dedicated to the Party, socialism and Communism." Whether Lei Feng ever existed or was the invention of Party propagandists was an open question. Whatever the case, newspapers in China still tirelessly regaled readers with paeans to this "model soldier."

Even though this was the most boneheaded kind of propaganda, I had always found Lei an intriguing phenomenon. There was something about his earnest, one-dimensional obsequiousness to the Party that made his alleged diary, the liturgical source for his hagiography, a wonder of political naivete. My first bonding experience with this canonized Communist saint came during my 1975 trip to China when our group was taken to an exhibit in the Shanghai Youth Palace that boasted a display of items purportedly from Lei's selfless life. Museum cases in this cupolaed 1920s building displayed many wonders, such as Lei's toothbrush, wash pan, sneakers, and even a pair of his underwear! These artifacts gave Chinese audiences the thrill of viewing a CCP version of a reliquary like those found in European cathedrals, where strands of hair, bone fragments, or toenail clippings from ancient saints are kept as holy relics. However, as our group left this Shanghai Lei Feng exhibit, a guide slyly confided to me that these revolutionary artifacts were actually only "facsimiles" (复制品). Of course, if Lei himself never really existed before being allegedly and ingloriously killed by a falling telegraph pole, how could they have been anything else?

That was the 1970s, when there were still many believers in Mao's revolution. But now, in the 1990s, when the Chinese were consumed by reformism, materialism, entrepreneurialism, capitalism, and cynicism, how could the Party ever expect the campy "spirit of Lei Feng" to compete?

■ ■ ■

In 1990, two Tsinghua University graduates were given respective sentences of eleven and fifteen years for criticizing the Party. "In February and March 1990 the defendants Chen Yanbin and Zhang Yafei worked in collusion to draft the reactionary journal *Iron Currents*," read an official statement about their case. They "attacked and slandered the leadership of the Chinese Communist Party," calling it "a forty-year-old authoritarian empire," and decried Mao's socialism as a "disaster and retrogression of mankind in the twentieth century." As a result of their attacks on the Party, the two Tsinghua students were charged with "inciting the masses to overthrow the political power of the people's democratic dictatorship and the socialist system" and imprisoned.

Such verdicts made it difficult to imagine how reforms, no matter how deep, could ever fully wash away China's autocratic Maoist mindset. They also set me thinking about the PRC's unique autocracy: In truth, China's brand of Leninism dovetailed all too neatly with its own millennial tradition of Legalism (法家), an ancient school of autocratic statecraft that sought to maintain order by means of a regimen of strict punitive responses to any kind of insubordination. By marrying foreign Leninism to indigenous Legalism, the Party had created a new strain of vigorous hybrid authoritarianism that was both local and imported, making it all the more difficult to extirpate.

Hinting at how deeply rooted this autocracy had become, not long after Deng Xiaoping began his bold reform movement in late 1978, he also announced "The Four Cardinal Principles" (四个基本原则), calling on Chinese to "uphold the Communist path, the people's democratic dictatorship, the leadership of the Chinese Communist Party, and Mao Zedong Thought and Marxism-Leninism." At the time, this announcement seemed so out of step with Deng's dramatic reforms that it was largely ignored. However, it was an important reminder, for those alert enough to read it correctly at the time, that no matter how bold reforms sometimes seemed, "Marxism-Leninism-Maoism" (马克思列宁毛主义/马列毛主义) was not going to be abandoned anytime soon. Why? Because it was the theological basis that justified the CCP's one-party system of control.

■ ■ ■

"I know there's a story here," Gelber began when we spoke a few days later. "But I also know that every *60 Minutes* program needs an interesting on-camera character. So we're going to have to find someone who not only knows what he's talking about, because he's been there, but can effectively guide viewers into a narrative."

"And, someone who, if caught, won't be afraid of going back to jail in the very gulag we're seeking to expose," I responded snidely. Gelber did not reply.

That very day, the Hong Kong press reported that new instructions on securing MFN status from the United States had been delivered by Deng himself at a Politburo meeting in Beijing: "Fight for MFN with the greatest of effort," he reportedly urged. "But, be ready to make necessary compromises, while at the same time being prepared for the worst and to make parallel counter moves."

Deng's declaration suggested a certain realism. China was becoming so intertwined with the global marketplace, it was hard to imagine how it could retreat back into the kind of autarky Mao once promoted as "self-reliance" (自力更生). China's economy was already so dependent on exports that it really did need ongoing MFN status to continue growing. However, there were myriad contradictions standing in the way of a fuller integration into the global economy. Prisons and forced labor, which bespoke the political differences between autocracies and democracies, were still causing real friction.

After Assistant Secretary of State for East Asian and Pacific Affairs Richard Solomon arrived in Beijing and touted the fact that the United States had succeeded in "institutionalizing" a dialogue on human rights with the Chinese government, I thought to myself, "We'll see." Chinese officials loved dialogue, because it gave the appearance of activity. But all too often their dialoguing led nowhere, except to more dialogue. With the Chinese, it was easy to get dialogued to death.

■ ■ ■

As spring 1991 unfolded, three more pro-democracy movement activists were sentenced in Xian for "counterrevolutionary incitement": Li Guiren, an editor at the Huayue Publishing House, received five years; Mao Hongliang, a student who headed the Shanxi Province Students' Autonomous Federation, received four; and Peng Ditang, a leader in the Xian Workers Autonomous Federation, received three. At the same time, in Beijing, a notice posted outside the Intermediate People's Court announced that twenty-four-year-old Han Weijun, accused of torching an armored personnel carrier on June 4, 1989, had been executed for "causing the state to suffer a financial loss of 220,000 RMB."

Reading such news items always made me wonder who these people actually were. Why had they been protesting? How had they been arrested? Did they have spouses and children? What would their periods of imprisonment be like? Did they have any regrets about what they had done? When I mentioned these cases to Gelber, he exclaimed, "These are exactly the kinds of people we should try to focus on!"

As a writer, I had long since learned how frustratingly difficult it was to imbue such cases with any vividness. Since journalists were not allowed to speak with detainees or prisoners, and since relatives and friends were usually too terrified by threats of retribution to speak in their stead, it was difficult to do anything more than pass on the basic facts provided in minimalist form by state media outlets. By tightly controlling news and information, the Party managed to prevent any victim's case from becoming a "story," exactly what Gelber wanted for *60 Minutes*. Finding ways to individualize some of these actual cases was not going to be easy.

■ ■ ■

When U.S. Rep. Frank Wolf, a Republican Congressman from Virginia, and Rep. Chris Smith, a Republican from New Jersey, took a congressional delegation to China in February, the question of Chinese prison forced labor popped up. Rep. Smith was a devout Catholic who openly acknowledged that his faith influenced his commitment to defending human rights in the U.S. Congress, where he had become an uncompromising critic of China's rights record.

While in Beijing, Smith and Wolf's delegation was taken to the model penitentiary, Beijing No. 1 Prison, a facility to which foreigners had long been escorted almost as if it were a unique living museum. In fact, as early as 1961, the prison was being touted to foreign visitors as one of the wonders of China's socialist penal system. And many innocents, especially leftists eager to be impressed by the tonic effects of Mao's Communist revolution, came away extolling it as a socialist model.

In his heartbreaking 1974 remembrance, *Prisoner of Mao*, Jean Pasqualini, who was half Chinese and half French and had spent years locked up in PRC prisons, identified Beijing No. 1 as "one of the best attractions for the standard Beijing tour of foreign visitors," whom he described as reacting to such prisons "predictably," if naively. "How many pages of emotional praise have I read since my release concerning the wisdom and humanity of the Chinese prison system, all of them due to the good offices of Beijing No. 1 Prison," he sardonically wrote.

During their own tour, Wolf and Smith were graced with a tour of the prison's textile and shoe plants, where they were surprised to see piles of stockings embroidered with figures of pandas playing golf tagged with English language labels. When asked if these "Double Golden Horse Brand" stockings were being sold abroad, prison officials insisted that the "goods made in this prison are not for export." The denial seemed highly spurious.

■ ■ ■

March had just begun when the editor-in-chief of the overseas edition of *The People's Daily*, Shao Huaze, came under investigation by the ministries of Public Security and State Security. This flagship Party mouthpiece aimed at Chinese living abroad had just published a seemingly harmless poem entitled "Lantern Festival." However, sleuths quickly discovered that if the poem was read diagonally from the top right to the bottom left corner, it contained an embedded message: "Li Peng Must Step Down to Appease the Hatred of the People" (李鹏下台平民恨).

Li Peng was the Chinese premier blamed for taking a hard-line approach against the Tiananmen Square protest movement, leading to the Beijing Massacre. A mole had not only somehow insinuated this subversive line into this paean to the Lantern Festival but gotten it placed in one of the Party's most exalted propaganda organs, one that sought to present China to the world in a roseate light.

It is, of course, any nation's sovereign prerogative to decide what rules govern its media. But the CCP's extreme sensitivity to criticism suggested how deep the Chinese leadership's fear of being publicly embarrassed was. This sensitivity came partially from China's history of powerlessness to defend itself against the predations of technologically superior foreign "great powers" that had bullied, exploited, occupied, colonialized, imperialized, and looked down on China as "the sick man of Asia" (东亚病夫) during the second half of the nineteenth and early part of the twentieth centuries. This narrative of victimhood, aggrievement, and humiliation had become the basis of Lenin's theories on imperialism that, once adopted by the CCP, were amplified by relentless waves of Party propaganda to become so deeply rooted in the collective psyche of the Chinese people that they endured even as the power balance began changing radically in China's favor during the 1980s and China's economic boom.

Even after President Richard Nixon and his national security adviser, Henry Kissinger, visited Beijing in 1972 and took the first steps toward the policy that ultimately became known as "engagement," this narrative of aggrievement did not end. Neither did the CCP's deep and abiding neuralgia against being humiliated abroad nor its animus against foreign pressure and criticism of the Chinese government's treatment of its own citizens on such matters and the universal nature of democratic and human rights. Control of the press, even if it involved violating Article 35 of China's own constitution, which "guarantees citizens freedom of speech, of the press, of assembly, of association, of procession, and of demonstration," was viewed as essential to maintain order and China's sense of national dignity.

A recent article in the English-language weekly *Beijing Review* described the CCP's stance this way: "First, there are no universal and abstract human rights. . . . Countries with different ideologies and social systems and at different stages of development have different understandings of the basic concept of human rights." Second, the article emphasized, since there are no universal human rights, they "cannot override the laws of various countries," because "international documents relating to human rights do not supersede the laws of any country."

By denying that rights derived from universal values, the Party was able to reject the notion that rights were part of a global commons shared by all human beings from birth. Instead of viewing all people as equally endowed with certain unalienable rights, the Party viewed rights as class-based. Those born into worker or peasant families, for example, were viewed as members of "the proletariat" and thus possessing rights. However, those born into families of landlords, businessmen, bankers, or other professional classes were deemed members of "the bourgeoisie" and thus not entitled to such rights.

By rejecting the notion of universal human rights, the Party was thus conveniently also able to reject the idea that journalists—domestic or foreign—possessed the right to report unfettered, no matter where they might be working. In many ways, the Cold War was driven by these two fundamentally different views of how rights were conceptualized under communism and democracy.

During the heyday of Deng's reform era, many U.S. diplomats, legislators, and even some rights defenders were willing to overlook ongoing abuses as long as China continued to "reform," "open up," and make progress, however haltingly, toward a more universal rights-based system. But, then came the Beijing Massacre, the rollback of political reform, and the collapse of the Soviet Union. The increments of tolerance that had been gained during the reform years began to be greatly constricted.

U.S. President George H. W. Bush had been inclined, during the late 1980s and even early 1990s, to indulge Beijing as a way to "maintain the relationship." He hoped that increased interaction would somehow goad China back onto a pathway that would slowly render it more convergent with U.S. interests and the existing global order.

Having lost the Soviet Union as a common threat binding the two nations together, in the 1990s, President Bill Clinton sought to revive the idea of détente with a new operating system that ultimately became known as "engagement." Its fundamental assumption was that more trade, investment, and cultural exchange would create a common interest that might enable both countries to continue overlooking the still stark political differences that divided them and thus maintain a reasonably stable relationship.

However, with the enthronement of Xi Jinping in 2012–13, tendencies that had already started to manifest themselves under his predecessor, Hu Jintao, started moving in a distinctly retrograde direction. It was not long before the United States and China were drifting back into an increasingly hostile, neo–Cold War style of oppositional geopolitical relationship. All too soon, "decoupling" (脱钩) had become the watchword of the hour.

As the United States and China became increasingly estranged, the elusive question of what the limits of foreign intervention should be, especially toward a country like China that was so allergic to intrusive foreign criticism, was soon rearing its head, and in ever more antagonistic ways. Should the wrongs the CCP committed in China against its own people become the business, even the responsibility, of Americans and other outsiders? Who anointed international human rights observers as transnational watch dogs, especially over countries that eschewed the very notion of universal rights? Why should what happened inside a country like China not remain its exclusive affair, challengeable by its own people alone?

If a nation could be justifiably accused of interfering in the internal affairs of another sovereign nation over the question of rights, what about the kind of interference that was implicit in the work of foreign media outlets, universities, think tanks, human rights organizations, and economic consulting firms that did due diligence on Chinese companies as investment prospects, especially when done from inside China? Had they the right to explore and expose weaknesses and abuses?

In the case of the foreign media, these questions could be especially sensitive. For instance, did not the posting of resident correspondents in Beijing and Shanghai to do investigative research and then publish critical articles constitute a form of foreign interference? With regard to our own project, did CBS have the right to dispatch a secret team of investigative journalists to China to sneak around with cameras and expose human rights abuses in its labor camp system?

Our highly intrusive *60 Minutes* project made me think more and more about such questions. Of course, how one answered them depended on how one viewed the universal nature of rights. Did human beings have the right, perhaps even the obligation, to protect the welfare of other human beings, regardless of national boundaries? When people were arrested for speaking out or criticizing their own governments and were unable to defend themselves, did those who retained their freedom not have some duty to help them? In biblical terms, were we, in fact, our brothers' keepers? Is this not what the United Nations meant when it passed the "Responsibility to Protect" resolution in 2005, which overrode a state's sovereignty in order to prevent crimes against humanity?

As a means of promoting democracy, and sometimes attaining other objectives as well, the United States had imposed temporary or partial trade and investment bans on some seventy-seven occasions since World War II. Perhaps the most notable instance was against South Africa's apartheid system in 1986. Such precedents made me wonder what a jailed Chinese dissident might think upon learning that the U.S. government had committed itself to using pressure to gain the release of political prisoners in South Africa, but refused to use the same tools on behalf of political prisoners in China, where abuses were even more widespread.

■ ■ ■

While waiting in California for *60 Minutes* to decide on Gelber's program idea, I started paying closer attention to how the issue of forced labor was playing in the debate in the U.S. Congress over the renewal China's MFN trade status. Beijing's attitude was clear: Chinese leaders wanted MFN renewal and were aggressively lobbying for its passage.

However, they had no stomach for forthrightly addressing the forced labor issue.

Sun Zhenwu, director of the American and Pacific Department of the Ministry of Foreign Economic Relations and Trade (MOFERT), warned that revocation of China's MFN status would not only harm mutual economic interests and bilateral relations between the United States and China but would also affect the stability and prosperity of Hong Kong. He argued that because of its reliance on entrepot trade from China, the colony stood to lose $10 billion if preferential trade status for China was revoked.

By emphasizing how dependent Hong Kong was on the outcome of the debate, Beijing officials evidently hoped to improve the chances that a favorable bill would make it through the U.S. Congress. Of course, it was not really out of concern for the people of Hong Kong that they raised this point. Their concern was more self-interested and transactional: Because they knew Americans were far more sympathetic toward the British colony than Beijing, they emphasized its potential losses.

The deepening negative sentiment in the United States toward China had not immediately affected trade or investment, but it was a reminder that the unresolved differences between the two political systems had the capacity to eventually impact even their economic and trade relations.

If one reminded a Chinese official that many Americans were turned off by Beijing's autocratic tendencies, their default response was that such negative attitudes were simply a form of unprovoked Western prejudice, what they referred to as an "outdated Cold War mentality" (过时的冷战思维). They did not accept that such views were something the Party itself had helped create with its own policies and behavior and thus actually also had the power to remedy. This blindness was the result of the Party's own narrative of victimization, with its signature notion of "a hundred years of national humiliation" (百年国耻), deeply steeped in the supposition that colonialization and imperialization had caused the lion's share of China's ills. This conclusion grew out of the belief that the Chinese people had been arbitrarily and unjustly acted upon by innately hostile imperialist outside forces at a time when they were largely powerless to retaliate.

It was not that this narrative had no truth, but by encouraging it as a default reaction even as China was beginning to enjoy an economic boom and gaining the means to defend itself, leaders were deprived of a counternarrative that would allow them to feel less besieged and more able to control their own destiny. But that required leaders like Xi to continue reforms, lessen animosity with the United States, and restabilize the relationship with the United States and other key partner countries by being less blameful. Instead, Chinese leaders remained stuck in an endless blame game in which each revelation against them led to another round of denials and counterattacks on critics. It was a depressing circle of defensive self-abasement in which Chinese leaders forfeited their own considerable abilities to remedy the reality. Perhaps most deleterious, the PRC's actions made too many other countries that actually shared common interests with China and wanted to get along feel threatened and insecure.

Here Chinese leaders had something to learn from Shakespeare when, in *Julius Caesar*, he deputized Cassius to lament to Brutus, "Men at some time are masters of their fates: The fault, dear Brutus, is not in our stars, but in ourselves." This drumbeat of self-defeating Chinese behavior continued throughout the first quarter of 1991.

■ ■ ■

Another such example reared its incriminating head on a goodwill trip to China by an American Bar Association (ABA) delegation in April. One of the delegation's stops was the Shanghai No. 1 Prison, another "model socialist" facility to which visitors were often taken in hopes of convincing them that the PRC's penal system was far more humane than it was usually depicted by foreign media.

A Chinese white paper, "Criminal Reform in China," that had been recently published as part of an effort to counter foreign allegations that torture, hunger, and forced labor were common in its *laogai* system, claimed that "after the founding of the People's Republic, the people's government established a new kind of socialist prison, where the prisoners are regarded as human beings, where their dignity is respected, their personal safety is insured and they receive fully humane treatment."

After touring a production line at Shanghai No. 1 Prison, ABA delegates met with the deputy warden. When ABA president John. J. Curtin asked where the goods made in their prison factory were sold, he was assured they were sold only in domestic markets. However, just before the delegation departed the prison, they happened to pass through a production area where the roving eye of Curtin's wife, Mary, spotted something that piqued her interest: Seagram's logos inscribed on a stack of cardboard boxes. When she asked prison officials if she might have a sample, they became agitated, refused her request, denied these cartons were for export, and hastily squired the delegation away from the area. As it turned out, sharp-eyed Mary Curtin had spotted packaging made for Seagram's wine cooler by prisoners who had carelessly, or perhaps intentionally, left their handiwork out in plain view of this visiting delegation.

"We are an innocent party," claimed the manager of Shanghai Seagram's Ltd., Philip Leung, when questioned about the incident. "Without our knowledge, subcontracting was done at the prison the ABA visited." Another Seagram's spokesman, Robert Kasmire, later explained to the press that when Seagram's headquarters heard the news that boxes printed with their logo had been found in Shanghai No. 1 prison, the company ended what it called "that relationship."

Seagram's may have belatedly terminated its subcontract, but who knew how many other foreign companies or buyers continued to have supply lines that unwittingly, or wittingly, reached back into Chinese prison facilities using force labor?

■ ■ ■

On my virgin trip to China in 1975, the veneration many on our delegation, notably its leftist American leaders, showed for whatever our official hosts chose to show or tell us, especially officials in the Shanghai prison, was notable. Their censorious attitude toward those American "comrades" who were inclined to ask probing questions reminded me of something Alexander Solzhenitsyn had just written in his *Gulag Archipelago*, quoting a *Life* magazine article penned by leftist New York State Supreme Court Judge Samuel S. Leibowitz, who had once visited Stalinist Russia on tour.

"What an intelligent, far sighted humane administration from top to bottom!" the U.S. judge had rhapsodized after visiting a model Soviet prison in 1958. "In serving out his term of punishment, the prisoner retains a feeling of dignity."

Solzhenitsyn mockingly commented, "Oh, fortunate New York State, to have such a perspicacious jackass for a judge!"

In a warning to those who had traipsed through other model socialist correctional facilities, Solzhenitsyn acidly added, "And oh, you well fed, devil-may-care, near-sighted, irresponsible foreigners with your notebooks and ball point pens. . . . How much you have harmed us in your passion to shine with understanding in areas where you did not grasp a lousy thing!"

■ ■ ■

I myself have toured such model prisons in Beijing, Shenyang, and Shanghai. In 1975, when I was given a guided tour of Shanghai No. 1 Prison, I was on one of those trips of fawning American "progressives" that Solzhenitsyn had so mercilessly lampooned. What distinguished my group was that they were more concerned with "building friendship" (建立友谊) with Chinese Communist Party officials than asking any hard questions that might prove embarrassing to our official hosts, much less acknowledge what was before our very eyes.

Indeed, over the years I have come to cringe upon hearing the word *friendship* when uttered by Chinese officials. This was particularly true after repeatedly losing Chinese colleagues who had become real friends because of what I had written, although not about them. Sometimes their real friendship caused agents from the Ministry of State Security or the Ministry of Public Security to visit and warn them that further association with me would have deleterious consequences for them. While such visitations were benignly referred to as "being invited in for tea" (请喝茶), they were actually ominous signals that a person like me was under official surveillance for errant thinking and that further contact with would affect their future.

The experience of having friends interrogated and threatened on my account and then suddenly sever their relations with me and my wife out of fear was, for us and other foreign colleagues, profoundly disturbing. Not only did we lose real friends, we felt responsible for endangering them.

In one such instance, after a brilliant archeologist friend was "invited in for tea," he broke off his close relationship with us. Some months later, when we naively tried to make contact with him through a third party, the response that came back was terse: Please cease and desist further efforts to make contact. The experience was like having someone for whom you cared unexpectedly die.

Because friendship demands a different kind of loyalty than what is owed the Party or the state, in the upside-down world of the CCP true friendship came to be viewed as a form of noncompliance, an essentially subversive act, because it too often conflicted with loyalty to the Party. As the expression went, "The party comes first." Having thus undermined true friendship between individuals, the Party filled the void with its own version, a synthetic form of "friendship" that demanded near total allegiance to it and its leadership. In this transubstantiation, friendship was eviscerated of its most fundamental human attribute, namely as a form of fraternity between two individuals who genuinely like each other. Instead, the concept of friendship was expropriated by the Party and turned into a hackneyed meme for official use, as in the Chinese People Association for Friendship with Foreign Countries or the US-China People's Friendship Association, Party/government-mandated and -controlled organizations dedicated to ersatz Party-generated versions of friendship that treated the notion like a commodity that could be produced and quantified like bushels of soybeans or tons of coal.

The state notion of friendship became so corrupted that whenever a Chinese government officials smarmily referred to a foreigner as an "old friend of China" (中国的老朋友), many experienced it as a cringeworthy moment signaling that said "friend" had become a compliant and trustworthy lapdog of the Party.

Only once in my many decades in China did a ranking Party official ever deign to refer to me as "an old friend of China." But on that occasion, there were extenuating circumstances. I was accompanying the investor and philanthropist George Soros to a meeting with Zheng Bijian, the executive vice president of the Central Chinese Communist Party School in Beijing. At the time, in the early 2000s, Soros was still welcomed in China, and Zheng clearly wanted to cultivate him, his influence, and his philanthropy by winning him over with a little "friendship" display lobbed in my direction. So, even though other officials generally viewed me as an American writer and scholar "with an attitude problem" (有态度问题), Zheng smilingly, if transactionally, anointed me "an old friend of China" in front of Soros. I felt as if I had just won a Chinese version of the Stalin Peace Prize.

■ ■ ■

Even though Baifang was pregnant, she and I decided we would still go on a long-planned March trip to Moscow, the cradle of the Bolshevik Revolution, to visit my oldest friend, the writer Adam Hochschild, and his wife Arlie, another writer. Adam, who spoke Russian, was working in Moscow archives that had just been opened to foreigners as part of Gorbachev's *glasnost* and *perestroika* on a project about post-Soviet Russia's relationship to its past, especially its infamous gulag. He ultimately published a book in 1994, *The Unquiet Ghost: Russians Remember Stalin.*

As we prepared to depart for Moscow, news bulletins from China that I would have liked to ignore kept pouring in, so that sometimes I was beginning to feel I had metamorphosed into one of those species of bacteria that has evolved to thrive on toxic sludge! At a press conference in Beijing, Foreign

Minister Qian Qichen was asked if China was willing to have discussions on human rights with the United States. He answered:

> Some people say that human rights have no boundaries. This does not accord with the facts, because according to international law the realization and guarantee of human rights must be brought about through the domestic laws of various countries. So, naturally the principle of state sovereignty cannot be ruled out in this respect. For example, the U.S. has been advocating human rights, but so far it has failed to ratify the two most important international human rights covenants. It has failed to sign a series of human rights conventions, for example, on apartheid, racial discrimination, and the prohibition of torture and discrimination against women. The U.S. has been doing this on the grounds that human rights essentially fall under the domestic jurisdiction of each country and that some of the articles of the above-mentioned conventions conflict with the domestic laws of the U.S.

Score one for Minister Qian against American evangelism for the universality of human rights.

■ ■ ■

The phone rang at an ungodly hour the morning just before we were scheduled to depart for Moscow.

"Hewitt gave us a green light!" Gelber erupted.

Because he had such a positive head of steam up, I did not want to utter any immediate words of disparagement. But, because of Baifang's condition, his news actually flooded me with uncertainty. When, without any response from me, Gelber insisted we find a way to meet before our departure, all I could suggest was dinner in Los Angeles the next night as we transited LAX on our way from San Francisco to Moscow via Zurich. He said he would book plane tickets right away for him and his associate producer, Doug Hamilton, and make a reservation for 5:30 p.m. at the Encounter Restaurant on top of an iconic space-age structure that sits at the center of LAX terminals.

■ ■ ■

As soon as we entered the LAX restaurant and I saw Gelber's enthusiastic smile, I knew this was no time to start throwing cold water on his just approved project. Then, as we were eating dinner and discussing possible next steps, Baifang surprised us all: She offered to go to Beijing herself right after we returned from Russia to explore whether interviews with any former political prisoners could be arranged. Of course, she was well aware of the Chinese government's sensitivities to anyone—Chinese or foreign—who dared undertake any kind of investigative activities dealing with political prisoners. In China, because such inquiries were viewed as tantamount to subversion, her offer filled me with even more trepidation.

Even though she now had an American passport and knew how to operate with discretion, her bold and magnanimous offer and her unfailing loyalty as a wife took my breath away.

As she slept beside me on the way to Moscow that night, I found myself pondering not only the very different backgrounds and experiences that had shaped each of us, but the wonderous way we had somehow converged so well in marriage.

She had been born in north China just before her parents were "assigned" (插队) to separate work units in distant cities. So, as an infant, she was left with her penurious ironsmith grandfather and grandmother in the gritty city of Xinxiang in Henan Province, where she endured extremely difficult times. She almost starved to death as a four-year-old in 1960 after the Great Leap Forward, when Mao's precipitous communization of agriculture brought about one of the worst famines in human history.

Not until she was ten years old was she able to reunite with her parents in Beijing. But her arrival in the capital came just as the Great Proletarian Cultural Revolution was beginning and schools were shutting down. With Chinese society thrown into even more tumult, she was first "sent down" (下放) to work in a rural area outside Beijing, then assigned to a city transistor radio factory, and finally sent to perform in a propaganda dance troop (评剧团).

One thing that always mystified me about her: How had someone possessing such elegance, clarity of vision, and personal loyalty have emerged from the acid bath of Mao's revolution? While the Party was producing millions of submissive, sycophantic, opportunistic, and traitorous fellow travelers, extraordinary people like her were also somehow being forged. It was a question that I still have not answered.

Chapter Five

THE BETHLEHEM OF BOLSHEVISM

IN ITS FALLEN STATE of Communist grace, by the end of the twentieth century Moscow was no longer the epicenter of world socialism it had once been during the heyday of Stalinism and the Comintern, a Soviet organ that promoted, aided, and coordinated activities of Communist parties and revolutions around the world. Nonetheless, once in Moscow, I did have the feeling of having arrived in the Bethlehem of Communism. In spite of all the Slavic architecture and Russian Orthodox churches that dotted the cityscape, there was much about this capital of the former USSR that was familiar to pilgrims like us from the People's Republic of China. Beijing still had enough residue left over from its reckless ideological fling with Moscow under Stalin during the 1950s to make us feel somewhat at home.

When the two Communist titans signed the Sino-Soviet Treaty of Friendship, Alliance, and Mutual Assistance in 1950, a gusher of Russian aid, architecture, and military assistance turned on that left Beijing marked with a host of clunky Russian-style landmark buildings whose presence still memorialized this moment of transnational socialist fraternity. The old Beijing Railway Station, the Exhibition Center, the Museum of the Chinese Revolution, the Great Hall of the People, and the Friendship Hotel, once the largest buildings in Beijing, were all designed and built by the Soviets. Festooned with hammers and sickles chipped into stone facades and garnished with kitsch socialist statues of defiant proletarians filled with Marxist-Leninist fervor, they harkened back to Moscow and the Stalin era.

And not to be forgotten, even though it ended up outdoing Moscow's Red Square in size, was that Tiananmen Square was also designed and constructed with Soviet assistance. This grand Russian-style plaza filled with heroic socialist monuments and surrounded by massive Russian-style buildings was created as a distraction from the grim reality of everyday Chinese life during Mao's revolution. Three decades after this transactional alliance ended with the bitter Sino-Soviet Rift in 1959, these stolid relics of "socialist solidarity" still lingered on as reminders of how quickly friends can become enemies.

Ever since I started studying China, I had been astonished by how difficult it was for people living in an open society to comprehend what living under a politically oppressive, autocratic regime was like. With the exception of recent immigrants, such systems remained abstractions rather than realities for most Americans. Perhaps only people who, like Solzhenitsyn, had actually been imprisoned in a gulag could understand the full measure of evil they incarnated and could thus decide to consecrate their lives to unmasking them. But China was still waiting for its Solzhenitsyn, someone whose bitter experiences converged with an unrepentant toughness and a sense of sarcasm and irony capable of giving their writing the same kind of biting power as Solzhenitsyn's three-volume epic on Russia's labor camps, *The Gulag Archipelago*, published in 1973.

As we toured Moscow, ever on my mind was the fact that this was the city in which Lenin and Stalin, borrowing from the czars, had perfected a new formula for shipping millions of Russian political dissidents off to their vast network of remote prison camps, many in distant Siberia. Of Bolshevism's many horrific contributions to the history of totalitarianism, this may have been its most monumental one. The Soviet gulag proved such an effective incarceration machine that Mao borrowed it from Stalin for his own newly fledged "people's republic," where its adoption in Sinofied form has endured ever since.

The book Hochschild was researching in Russia involved delving into how Russian-based nongovernmental organizations like Memorial understood the ongoing effects of the Soviet gulag on modern Russia. As part of his research, he had interviewed numerous survivors about their experiences in Stalin's camps during the 1930s and '40s. He had even traveled to Siberia to document some of the camps that made up the USSR's vast penal archipelago. By then, many were little more than snarls of rusting barbed wire fences, collapsing guard towers, derelict lagers, and weed-strewn prison yards. But

Hochschild stumbled onto one particularly horrifying relic of Stalin's gulag in Kolpashevo, along the Ob River in the oblast of Tomsk. He later wrote:

> Over the years the Ob River often changed its course. But recently the channel moved again and this time began to cut into an earthen embankment near an old prison that had become a mass grave in which inmates, some of whom had been executed on orders of the camp chief, were buried. But, upon interment, their bodies became frozen in the permafrost layer. There their frozen corpses remained in repose over the intervening decades. However, when the river bed shifted, the current of river began cutting into the embankment and some of these bodies were unearthed, floating downstream, and washing up on the banks of the river.

Hochschild told me that older people in Tomsk sometimes even recognized the still clothed bodies of former frozen prisoners as they thawed out and washed up on the river's banks downstream.

Here in Russia, China seemed both far away and close at hand. After all, a similar network of camps still stretched across China's 6,359-kilometer sweep from Kashgar in Xinjiang Province in the west to Wusu in Heilongjiang Province on the Siberian border to the east. And these camps were still filled with untold millions of political prisoners. As I listened to Hochschild recount his experiences working in Russia, it occurred to me that, just as bodies were reappearing along the Ob River in Siberia, the ghosts of the dead from China's reform-through-labor camps would also someday, figuratively speaking, resurface and demand atonement.

Many Chinese I talked to over the years were tempted to believe that the psychological impact of their own country's labor camps would somehow remain limited to those who were unfortunate enough to have been confined in them. That proposition always struck me as naive and dubious. For when a father, husband, mother, sister, or brother was suddenly taken away by secret police, his or her involuntary absence not only radiated throughout that family, but cascaded down through later generations in ways both subtle and profound. The traumatic effects of executions, starvation, purges, long imprisonments, parents separated from children, humiliations, and all the other indignities that had been heaped on the Chinese people, many in their most formative years, have kept replicating from fathers and mothers to sons and daughters, and finally to grandchildren.

Current Party Secretary General Xi Jinping was a case in point. He grew up in a family where his father, Xi Zhongxun, was twice purged, the second time for sixteen years as an "historical counterrevolutionary" (历史反革命分子). This happened just as his son was coming of age. Understandably, many Chinese have been reluctant to openly discuss these travails. What is the point of revisiting a past that can neither be changed nor for which any amends will be made? "Don't talk about such things!" (不要说了) is a common refrain when such subjects arise. And who would not want to put such historical traumas out of mind . . . if they can?

However, it would surprise me greatly if such horrors could so neatly be dismissed and forgotten. After all, tens of millions of victims and hundreds of millions more family members and friends were affected by Mao's endless political campaigns and struggles over the nearly half a century of his dominion over China's leadership. His repressiveness wrought an incalculable amount of physical and psychological damage on his people that they will not soon forget or overcome. Even though there has not yet been a public reckoning in China, the deep wounds left by this period of history will ultimately beg for one.

Part III

INTO THE HEART OF THE DRAGON

Chapter Six

GETTING STARTED

BY MID-APRIL, we had arrived back home from Moscow, but Baifang had to prepare almost immediately to leave again for Beijing. Her charge was to discreetly seek out former labor camp inmates and see if anyone might be willing to recount their prison experiences on camera, shot secretly and in silhouette to guard their anonymity. Although I had complete confidence in her, I still felt no small disquiet about her taking on this assignment. After all, she not only was pregnant but would be working alone. But there was something about being in Russia and hearing so much about the legacy of Stalin's camps from Hochschild that made her more determined than ever to take on this assignment. Her quiet inner strength, honed no doubt by having endured the most intense period of Mao's revolution herself, would, I hoped, serve her well in this undertaking. Still, even as her demonstration of loyalty and fidelity was touching, the prospect of her setting off alone was unsettling.

■ ■ ■

Two days before Baifang was to leave our peaceful ranch, a colleague at Stanford University rang me up. As we chatted, he asked me what I was up to. When I told him about our *60 Minutes* project, he too immediately expressed his skepticism. But then he brought up the name of a colleague at Stanford who, he said, had been a political prisoner in China for almost two decades. What is more, my friend said he was now busy compiling a documentary record of China's reform-through-labor camp system at the Hoover Institution on Peace, War and Revolution at Stanford. As he recalled, Wu Hongda 吴弘达, or Harry Wu, had been born in the late 1930s, one of many siblings in a prosperous Christian banking family in Shanghai whose wealth and standing were destroyed by Mao's revolution. After the 1956 Soviet invasion of Hungary, Wu had expressed some criticism of Moscow and had been arrested as a "counterrevolutionary rightist" (反革命右派) and then held in the PRC's *laogai* system for the next nineteen years. Upon being released in 1979, my friend believed, Wu had received an academic invitation from UC Berkeley's department of geology, his original field of study, and had managed to leave China.

As my friend was recalling what he knew about Wu, I suddenly realized that I had actually met him myself after a speech he had given at Columbia University. With a little rummaging on my desk, I even found the card he had given me at the time.

So, after finishing up with my friend, I called the number on Wu's card. When he picked up and I explained who I was, he recalled our Columbia meeting. But when I began explaining the *60 Minutes* project and asked if he still knew any people in China who had spent time in labor camps, he fell so silent that I felt foolish for having even asked the question.

"It's not that simple," he finally responded, but almost contemptuously. "Of course I have my networks of special friends there. But these are people who trusted each other implicitly, because of what we all went through together. We're bound by a very personal connection that's not transferable to anyone who wasn't inside with us. So, they'd be no use to you or CBS, even if I introduced you to them." Then, with an air of finality, he ended the conversation by saying, "Anyway, I just got married to a woman from Taiwan."

But before he could hang up, I managed to ask if he would be willing to meet with me the next day, when I would be dropping Baifang off at San Francisco International Airport for her trip to Beijing and then later boarding a flight to New York myself to meet with Gelber. He surprised me by agreeing.

■ ■ ■

When Wu and I met in the international terminal at SFO, I found a handsome man in his late fifties whose bespectacled eyes radiated both intensity and sadness. He willingly told me about his work at the Hoover Institution, where he was creating a Chinese-language database of the names, locations, and histories of as many reform-through-labor camps in China as he was able to document through his Chinese-language research. "I hope my work will give people in the outside world some idea of the *laogai* system's scope and scale," he explained. He also told me he had pledged not to rest until the Chinese word *laogai*, like Russia word *gulag*, "appeared in every language dictionary in the world."

When I pressed him again as to whether he still had contacts in China, he was no more forthcoming than before. And when I asked about the possibility of finding someone familiar with China's labor camp system who might be able to help us work with a hidden video camera, he again demurred. But then he stunned me.

"You know," he began in a very matter-of-fact way, "the one who should go back into the camps with a camera is really me."

"You mean you'd go back?" I asked incredulously.

"Well . . . I could," he smiled.

"But you might land right back in the camps again yourself!"

"Of course!" he admitted. "But don't forget, I know that world better than anyone, and I understand how to read almost every situation."

Since my flight for New York was about to leave, we had to break off our conversation at this very portentous moment. But, as I ran to my gate, wheels were spinning in my head.

Would Wu really risk going back?

Could he get into China?

If he did, could he actually get back into some of the reform-through-labor camps in which he had once languished?

Did he know how to use a video camera?

And, given the way post-1989 security forces were monitoring all dissident activity, could someone like him escape detection?

■ ■ ■

The following day, when I mentioned my conversation with Wu to Gelber and Hamilton at lunch in New York, both immediately snapped to attention.

"You mean, he's willing to go back himself?" exclaimed Gelber.

"It seems so," I responded. "But I'm far from sure he would succeed. He could very easily just get arrested again, and then we'd be in a real pickle."

However, both Gelber and Hamilton had already risen to the bait. Gelber wanted to return to their CBS office as soon as lunch was over to present this new possibility to Don Hewitt.

As the executive producer of *60 Minutes*, Hewitt presided over the legendary CBS News franchise as if he were a potentate ruling a small nation. The immense commercial success of *60 Minutes* had given him prerogatives few other television executives enjoyed. And nothing won his subordinates more praise than the promise of a dramatic, timely, exciting story. Conversely, nothing won his disapprobation faster than a project that had fallen apart, a budget that had ballooned, or a timely celebrity interview that had been lost to a competitor.

We found Hewitt in his West Fifty-Seventh Street CBS office behind a huge wooden desk with a fat cigar in his mouth.

"OK!" said Gelber, turning to me. "Tell Don what's at stake in this story."

"Well . . . ," I began, thinking fast. "With a debate boiling in the Congress over whether to reextend MFN status to China, any new documentation on China's prison system, or evidence of political prisoners engaging in forced labor to make goods that end up being illegally exported into the U.S., could be game-changing on the vote. Some in Washington want to sidestep the issue and continue to 'engage' China, hoping that our strained relations can be eased by more trade. But others believe that trading with a Marxist-Leninist regime like that in the People's Republic of China only lends support to an autocracy. Either way, the prison labor question is seminal. So . . . "

"OK," interrupted Hewitt. "Can we get tape? You know, like shots of prison camps and forced laborers at work?"

"Well . . . ," I hesitated.

"There's this Chinese guy named Harry Wu," Gelber interjected, evidently feeling the need to come to my rescue. "He's spent nineteen years in the camps. Schell talked with him and thinks we might get him to go back to China and . . . "

Hewitt's eye brows rose like a needle on a voltmeter charged with current.

"Sounds interesting," he said, stroking his chin.

"And, we . . . ," began Gelber.

"So, let's do it then!" interrupted Hewitt, wagging his cigar.

Chapter Seven

COLLABORATION

WHEN I CALLED WU to tell him that *60 Minutes* was interested in a prison labor story focusing on his own experience, he laughed.

Well, I've been talking to my new wife and . . . "

"And what?" I asked anxiously.

"And she says she'll never allow me to go back to China. She says I've suffered enough, and . . . " He did not finish.

However, as we continued talking, I sensed that, despite Wu's wife's dictum, he was reluctant to completely let go of this idea. And because I knew how disappointed Gelber and Hamilton would be, I procrastinated in telling them that Wu now seemed unwilling to participate.

■ ■ ■

The next morning, when I spoke with Wu again, I was surprised by what a font of thoughts, observations, and information on China's prison system he was. And, despite his wife's fiat, he seemed to still be bonded to this idea.

"Everyone knows about Nazi concentration camps and Stalin's gulag," he began. "But few outside China know anything about its system of prisons and forced labor camps, even though they've swallowed up millions like me."

Later, in an interview with the *Los Angeles Times*, Wu described these camps as "the cornerstone of the Chinese Communist dictatorship and the machinery for crushing human beings physically, psychologically and spiritually."

As we concluded this conversation, Wu's apparent willingness to stay engaged made me want to play things out a little more.

▪ ▪ ▪

Baifang called from Beijing the next night on what she said was a "secure" line. She told me that while she had met a few people who had served time in camps, none were willing to talk about their experiences publicly. But then, she added, "You know, part of the challenge for a project like this is deciding what actually constitutes 'imprisonment.' I mean, what's the difference between an 'educated youth' (知识青年) pulled out of a family and 'sent down' (下放) to the countryside in a remote part of China to do manual labor for ten years, an official sent off to a rural May 7th Cadre School (五七干校) for reeducation, and someone like Wu, who got put into a series of 'reform thru labor camps' for two decades?

"We Chinese love our hierarchies," she laughed. "We want to 'classify' everything. So, we have ideological retraining facilities, detention centers, jails, prisons, reeducation-through-labor camps, reform-through-labor camps, etc., each with its own name and rank. But, if we're honest, under Mao wasn't China just one huge prison camp?"

■ ■ ■

Even after another day of discussions with Wu, I was still unable tell whether he was pulling out or edging back into this project. But each time we spoke, I learned a more about him.

He had a deeply Catholic father, a loving stepmother who committed suicide after his arrest, and eight siblings, some of whom attacked their father after being manipulated and threatened by Maoist political activists. It was during his own nineteen years in prison that Wu decided he would dedicate his life to exposing the evils of the system of extrajudicial punishment under which he had suffered . . . if he ever got out! And, he said, his tenacity had only been strengthened by his years in prison. So, rather than being daunted by all the challenges and risks of the project we were proposing, he seemed energized by them.

Still, something continued to be elusive about his responses that made me reluctant to ask him outright to make a decision. There was perhaps another reason for my reluctance: I feared his answer. What would I do if he said, yes? Honestly, part of me was relieved by his standoffishness, because of my own ambivalence about getting more deeply involved. For if Wu did suddenly agree to team up with *60 Minutes*, the dangers for all of us would be enormous. What is more, since he had already spoken out in public, testified before the U.S. Congress, and established a reputation in the United States as an outspoken critic of China's prison system, the Party knew all about him and most certainly viewed him as a traitor who had sold out his Chinese birthright to "hostile foreign forces."

What made matters even more dangerous for him was that, although he had been living in the United States for almost six years, he still did not have an American passport. All he had was "landed U.S. immigrant status," entitling him to a "green card." Because he was still a PRC citizen, if he was picked up by authorities in China, American diplomats would not be able to intercede on his behalf. And making matters even more problematic was another vexing detail: Wu told me that his Chinese passport had expired. However, he valiantly insisted that his green card made him eligible for a U.S. "reentry permit," a courtesy travel document given by the U.S. government to immigrants who did not yet have citizenship, but had green cards. That temporary document would at least enable him to apply for a visa to China and then reenter the United States upon his return. And, he noted, one virtue of not using a Chinese passport was that with his U.S. reentry permit he was able to use his English name, Harry Wu, rather than his Chinese name, Wu Hongda. If he were on a blacklist back in China, which was not unlikely, the PRC visa office in Hong Kong and Chinese immigration authorities at the border might not have cross-referenced his two different names.

■ ■ ■

The next day, at Gelber's urging, I finally phoned Wu and put the question to him.

"You know," he began very softly, but then came a long pause. "In my mind's eye I've never been able to stop seeing prisoners in faded blue uniforms trudging off to work."

"What do you mean?" I probed.

"I mean that I'll never be able to set my nineteen years in those camps aside and just forget about my fellow prisoners."

"So?"

"So . . . I'll go back and see what I can do." He laughed nervously. I was speechless.

But as I thought more about his decision, it came to seem less and less surprising. Reform-through-labor camps had become his life. And, as he later wrote, "The Communist Party would tolerate only those who tucked their tails between their legs and bowed before its absolute authority. I could not do that." Now he intended to arch his back against the Party's absolute authority and pitch in with *60 Minutes* to defy it . . . in whatever ways he could.

"Way to go!" exclaimed Gelber ecstatically when I called him with the news. "This is going to be an incredibly important story!"

I did not disagree. But exactly how we were going to pull it all off continued to elude me.

Chapter Eight

UNTO THE BREACH

"IN CASE something happens to me in China, I've made out a will," Wu soberly announced when we next spoke.

This dark thought caught me off guard. But, jolted into being more mindful of what was at stake, I suggested that we do an on-camera interview with him before he left for China. That way, if he was detained, we would at least have a video testament ready to air in his defense. An interview would also give him a chance to explain why, after so much suffering, even escaping his homeland, he was willing to risk everything by going back to his old prison camps.

■ ■ ■

With a CBS camera crew set up at an old World War II gun emplacement in the shadow of the Golden Gate Bridge, Wu explained why he had decided to risk returning to his homeland. He referred to this shoot as his "last will and testament."

"Even though I wanted to forget the suffering of the past after arriving in the United States and even as I wanted to heal the wounds in my heart, the nineteen years of sorrow would not stop returning to my mind, I could not forget what I'd experienced or those who still suffer inside the camps," he began as the camera whirred. "If I didn't undertake this task, who would?"

After we finished the shoot, he handed me a fuller text for safekeeping.

"If I don't come back," he announced, "I'd like you to distribute this to the media."

> Twelve years ago, I left my last labor camp, the state-run Wang Zhuang Coal Mine located in the mountains of Huo County, Shanxi Province. When the small truck on which I'd thrown my belongings was about to depart, I gazed out over the dark valley and gave a long sigh. Nineteen bitter years as a prisoner in these labor camps had finally come to an end.
>
> As the truck began to move, I heard a distant rumble; how familiar that sound was to me. It was the sound of a coal cart emerging from the mine elevator and crashing into a hopper, where it discharged its contents. My eyes rested for a moment half way up the hillside where a long line of stooped and blackened figures were straining against their coal carts, inching slowly forward, just as I had done. Incessant echoes — crash-bang, crash-bang, crash-bang — filled the narrow valley . . .

By a great stroke of good fortune, I had now managed to get out of the reform-through-labor camp system, a vast prison machine that crushes all vestiges of humanity—not only flesh and blood, but spirit and ideas as well. And, since my departure the wheels of this grim apparatus have by no means ceased to turn. In the Soviet Union, the gulag system put in place by Stalin gradually fell apart after his death. But in China, the labor camps of the Mao Zedong era continue to flourish, even under Deng Xiaoping.

When I left the camps, my status was that of a "counter-revolutionary rightist" who had been "reinstated" by the authorities. I was accordingly assigned to return to my former university teaching post. But, when I got back there, I discovered that the former Anti-Rightist Campaign heroes, who would betray even their parents for the sake of the Party and Chairman Mao, were now in leading positions as officials with power and privilege who were held in the highest esteem. They cordially welcomed me back to join them in the struggle for Deng Xiaoping's Four Modernizations. However, at the same time, they showed not a hint of remorse about what they had done previously, which was their way of informing me that from now on, I would be expected to keep my tail between my legs. Indeed, it became quite clear to me that I was now only in a slightly larger cage than before . . .

In 1985 I finally succeeded in breaking my way out of that cage by coming to America. After all that I had been through, what I wanted most was just to somehow forget the nightmares of my past, and erase the brand that had been stamped on my heart. My wish was to lead a kindly, peaceful, and happy life, and before long I had my own little house, the respect of the people around me and a wonderful marriage that once I would never have dreamed possible. I was, in fact, living like a normal human being.

But some things refuse to be dissipated by a wave of the hand. The experiences of nineteen years in the camps kept streaming back into my mind. How could I forget them? How could I turn my back on what I had witnessed? And so, in 1987 I stopped working in my profession, geology, and took up a special research project at Stanford University's Hoover Institution.

Then, on June 4, 1989, tanks rolled onto Tiananmen Square and smashed the illusions held by many people about the Chinese Communist Party's program of "openness and reform." Deng Xiaoping's true and terrible face was vividly depicted in the fresh blood of the people of Beijing. But what we must realize is that those actually murdered at Tiananmen Square were only a tiny fraction of the people who have been arrested and thrown into labor camps over the past forty-odd years. China's notion of laogai, or "reform-through-labor," is the concept that underlies the largest concentration camp system in human history, and it is the cornerstone of Chinese Communist dictatorship.

Although writing two books has in some measure fulfilled my wish to introduce the world to the workings of the labor camp system, I feel that these efforts are still far from adequate. Returning to the mainland holds great dangers for me, not the least of which are the possibilities of losing once more the freedom and happiness that were so hard to come by in the first place, and causing my beloved wife to endure a lifetime of sadness and pain.

But still the sounds from the mine in my ears seem to ask, "Who will go?" And the answer that comes back is, "If I don't go, then, who will?"

■ ■ ■

A few days later, Baifang landed safely back from Beijing, allowing me to heave a sigh of relief.

"I talked to a lot of people," she began, as I drove her home. "Several were possibly willing to give anonymous interviews, but only for print and only if they were not identified by name. I didn't meet anyone willing to go on camera and tell their story, especially for a large American TV network." Then, sensing my disappointment, she added, "However, we might find a few Chinese now living in this country who've largely cut their ties with China who'd be willing to talk. But remember, almost everyone has relatives and friends back home who'd be put at risk. So even these people will be few."

Holding family members hostage has long been one of the Party's most effective ways of silencing those who have gone abroad to study, work, or live. Every Chinese knows that if they speak out while abroad, kith and kin will pay a price at home.

■ ■ ■

"There's something new I need to tell you!" Wu announced with a mixture of urgency and gleefulness just a few days later.

Whereas he had been rather standoffish in earlier conversations, now that we were formally in partnership, his reserve had begun to dissolve.

"What's up?" I asked.

"When I go back to China, I'm going to go with my new wife, Chen Ching-li!"

"But why?" I asked, stunned he would even think about taking his new Taiwan-born bride with him on such a dangerous mission. I mean, who takes a second honeymoon in the Chinese gulag?

"Last night she sat me down and told me that if this project is something I feel I really must do, she'll not only understand, but help me, because we are now man and wife."

"But, wouldn't that make it doubly risky for you?"

"No, because, if we go together, we'll look like just another ordinary tourist couple from Taiwan. And, by doing everything legally, should something happen, I can insist I wasn't breaking any laws, just showing my new wife my old life."

"But . . . "

"So, I don't want to use any fake papers, false names, or tell any lies," Wu interrupted. "We'll go openly as ordinary tourists and book our hotels and flight reservations through normal travel agents and that way reduce the risk that Chinese officials will suspect anything."

In the blink of an eye, he had transformed a dangerously covert operation into an overt one that would give him deniability, should he be picked up. It was a masterful plan!

■ ■ ■

I was relieved to find, as we got to know each other, that more and more of Wu's judgments impressed me as sensible. But what still made me wary was his near fanaticism about exposing what he viewed as the egregious inhumanity of China's reform-through-labor *apparat*. It was not that I thought he misjudged it, only that any fanatic is vulnerable to totalism. I surmised that this tendency emanated from having had his core shaped by all the time he had spent in extremis inside these very camps. His experiences there had no doubt combined with his innate sense of Catholic righteousness to make it almost impossible for him not to want to defy and resist the kinds of injustices that had been inflicted on him and were now being inflicted on so many others who remained in China. In this sense, Wu did indeed seem to share a common obsession with Solzhenitsyn.

For me, there was one perplexing question hovering over both men: How, after growing up in worlds where betrayal and treachery were so often the only pathways to survival, had they both developed such a sense of righteousness and such strong moral compasses? Had Christianity played a role? In Wu's case, his stubborn sense of conscience seemed to have developed through his strict Jesuit religious training. And in Solzhenitsyn's case, he became a devout Eastern Orthodox believer while in Russia's gulag.

■ ■ ■

California Representative Nancy Pelosi and her staff offered to help Wu obtain an expedited reentry permit, and as soon as it came through, he wanted to leave for Hong Kong, where he planned to apply for a tourist visa to China. If he got it, he wanted to go right in. He also told me that his code name would be "Peter," the name given him by the priests at St. Francis School in Shanghai who had initiated him into the church as a boy.

"While imprisoned, I often turned to God to survive," he diffidently explained.

■ ■ ■

Despite his usually no-nonsense manner, when we next talked, Wu seemed uncharacteristically rattled. I asked him if anything was wrong, and he reminded me that the anniversary of the June 4th Beijing Massacre was approaching.

"Things are reportedly very tense inside China," he began. "I wonder if I shouldn't delay my departure until after this politically sensitive anniversary has passed?"

I agreed that a delay made sense.

"Whenever I finally do go," he continued, "I have a plan that purposefully leaves whole periods of time unscheduled. That way, if I have to, I can change direction quickly, even send Ching-li home, and then just drop out of sight alone for a while. I want to make it as hard as possible for the authorities to follow or find me. I'm especially worried about being tracked through airline or train reservations that are all in a computer system."

If he was successful getting a China visa in Hong Kong, he told me, he planned to cross the border immediately and try to visit several of the camps in which he had once been imprisoned.

"Each camp has two names," he explained like a teacher. "The first name designates the camp as a penal institution, the second as a production unit. This distinction helps prison enterprises market their goods both at home and abroad, because having two names helps production facilities avoid any obvious association with prisons or forced labor."

Wu planned to start off at Qinghe Farm, also known as Beijing No. 1 General Reform-Through-Labor Detachment, where he was imprisoned twice. The camp, situated between the northern coastal city of Tianjin and Beijing, is a sprawling facility covering more than forty-four square miles of reclaimed agricultural land that still operates as a vast farm complex. Wu's first internment at Qinghe was during the post–Great Leap Forward famine in the early 1960s, when his body weight fell to seventy-two pounds. His second term was in 1967, during the high tide of the Cultural Revolution.

Next he planned to move on to Tuanhe Farm, or the Beijing No. 1 Reform-Through-Labor Detachment, outside Beijing, where he had been in solitary confinement and tortured. Then he would head to northwest China to the Wangzhuang Coal Mine, or the Shanxi No. 4 Reform-Through-Labor Detachment, near Taiyuan in Shanxi Province.

"The fact that I'm the first person who has dared to try and go back to these camps will be an advantage," he insisted.

"Why?" I asked.

"Because the guards won't be expecting such audacity and won't be on the lookout."

He also reminded me that he not only knew the geography of each of these camps well but also still had a few friends who had stayed on as "forced job placement personnel" (留场就业), former prisoners who, after their formal sentences ended, were still working inside the camps but living outside. He hoped that some of these old-timers would be able to help him gain entrance to the camps themselves, where he hoped to secretly shoot video with a camera rigged up to peek out of a hole in a seemingly harmless canvas shoulder bag.

Then Wu surprised me once again.

"Would you . . . " he began somewhat tentatively. "Would you be willing to follow me into China? I could use someone I trust working in parallel with me, someone who could take over whatever videotapes I manage to shoot so I won't have to go around with so much incriminating evidence. You could also restock me with fresh tapes, as well as just stand by in case anything bad happens? And, if anything happened to me, you could . . . "

With no small trepidation, I agreed.

■ ■ ■

The next morning at sunrise I was awakened by a jangling phone. Without even saying hello, Wu unleashed an avalanche of worries that had evidently been piling up in his mind that night. It seemed that he was now finally confronting the reality of actually going back to his old camps, and all sorts of long-suppressed memories, upsetting feelings, and fears were reawakening and agitating him.

"When I get back into those camps, I just hope I can control myself," he confided. "I've started to think not just about my time there, but also about my stepmother, my brother, and my father. They were all victims of the revolution and now are all gone. However, my stepmother's grave is still in Wuxi (无锡) and, if I can, I'd like to visit it with my wife." He choked up for a moment. "But I just hope I can control my feelings of outrage and revenge. I keep reminding myself that no matter what happens, I must remain calm, smile, and be nice. I can't afford to . . . " He was unable to continue.

"Tell me about your stepmother?" I asked.

"I was very close to her. But after I was arrested, in 1960, she committed suicide." He fell silent for another moment. "Well . . . I better get off now." His voice cracked with emotion.

After he hung up, the full import of what we were trying to do hit me, leaving me worried too, not just about him, but myself and Baifang. In a few days, I too was scheduled to leave for Hong Kong. Of course, my trip carried much less risk than his, because I had an American passport and whatever happened, I would probably be able to get home. Nonetheless, whatever lay ahead still filled me with anxiety.

I had visited China countless times over the past almost two decades, written about it extensively, and been actively involved with numerous official exchange programs as well as with many dissident Chinese intellectuals. However, I had never been engaged in a project as politically sensitive as this one. Although neither Wu nor I would be doing anything that was technically illegal, we both knew that if the Chinese government got wind of what we were up to, they would view it as a form of subversive undercover activity. Even if I was ready to accept the consequences myself, what about Baifang, who was Beijing-born? Although she was now an American citizen and we lived largely in the United States, the Chinese government had a tendency to view all people born in China as the "sons and daughters of the Yellow Emperor" (炎黃子孙), as subjects who, no matter what citizenship they actually held, somehow still belonged to China. Our activities could also have grave consequences for our friends and her parents.

Lastly, I was aware that she and I could end up being shut out of the country that had come to sit at the center of both our lives. Given what I had learned over the past few months researching the inner workings of China's public security apparatus and prison system, the regime was unforgiving and punitive toward people who intruded into forbidden realms.

▪ ▪ ▪

I was surprised when the president of the Beijing Foreign Correspondents Club (BFCC) called me first thing in the morning a few days before I was scheduled to travel to China. Somehow she had heard that I might be coming to Beijing, and she wanted to know if I would be willing to give a talk to the club's members. Since I had many colleagues in the Beijing foreign press corps and was always eager to interact with them, I groggily accepted her invitation.

The next morning, the phone rang again just after dawn. This time it was Wu. As soon as I picked up the receiver, he went off like a Roman candle, raising one alarming fear after another.

"Tomorrow's the anniversary of the June 4th Massacre, and anyone entering a university campus in Beijing is subject to a security check," he began without any felicitation. "They've even banned all youth gatherings until further notice, including a concert long planned in Beijing's Ritan Park (日坛公园) by Cui Jian" (崔健).

Cui, whom my wife and I knew, had become something of a bellwether for youth culture alienation trends in China. He came of age during Deng's reform era in the 1980s as a classical trumpeter in the Beijing Symphony Orchestra. However, by mid-decade, he had formed a rock band that included several foreigners, quickly making him a countercultural pioneer. Although Cui was not overtly political, his songs were critical in a satirical manner. In 1987, for example, he got into trouble with officials for spoofing an old revolutionary anthem, "Naniwan" (南泥湾). Then in 1989, his "Nothing to My Name" (一无所有) became a favorite of pro-democracy demonstrators. His song "Do it All Over Again" (从头再来) suggested that the 'golden road' of communism was coming to an end.

With their long hair and unorthodox dress, Cui's band members were the sartorial antithesis of the policelike lineups of Party elders tricked out in funereal black suits that showed up on the front page of the *People's Daily*. So it was hardly surprising that during such a sensitive anniversary, the leadership feared pop-culture iconoclasm almost as much as pro-democracy broadsides from dissident intellectuals. Unlike overt political dissidence, Cui's messages were oblique and culturally seductive, and thus harder for Party propagandists to challenge or control without opening themselves up to ridicule. So, whenever June 4th rolled around, paranoia abounded. As far as the Party was concerned, "every bush and each tree looked like an enemy soldier" (草木皆兵), as the old Chinese expression put it.

■ ■ ■

The day before I took off for Beijing to join Baifang, who was already there, she told me on the phone that the political atmosphere was tense. "Last night satellite transmissions for CNN and BBC were repeatedly interrupted in tourist hotels, as screens suddenly went black whenever news items on China came on," she reported.

I was scheduled, upon arrival, to address the Beijing Foreign Correspondents Club on the topic "The Silence of Chinese Intellectuals," a subject that had long interested me. Since all of the club's members were foreign and the meeting would be closed-door, I had blithely assumed the event would not give cause for much government attention. I had also convinced myself that this talk would be a good way for me to reconnect with members of the Beijing press corps, just in case anything happened to Wu and we suddenly needed some foreign media attention.

Chapter Nine

APPROACHING A RED-HOT STOVE

MY FLIGHT TO BEIJING was uneventful. Baifang met me at Capital Airport, and it was wonderful to be back at her side! Since we had been unable to speak openly on the phone, there was much she did not know about the progress of our project. So, as soon as we were safe in our car, she asked me for an update. When I told her that Wu, if he managed to get a visa in Hong Kong, would enter China with his wife in a couple of days, I saw a look of concern etch her face. But even though she was now almost five months pregnant, she did not protest.

When our cab arrived at the Palace Hotel, she had already checked in, so we went directly to our room. I had just fallen asleep when the phone rang.

"Yes," I answered only half awake.

"Hello!" an enthusiastic voice piped up.

"Who's this?" I demanded, irritated at being awakened.

"It's Peter calling from Hong Kong."

"Peter who?"

"You know! Peter!" the voice replied more stridently.

Only then did I remember that Peter was Wu's code name.

"Oh yes, Peter!" I replied, pretending I had known all along whom he was. But the fact I had let such an important detail slip my mind did not fill me with confidence in my ability to operate covertly.

"How are your contract negotiations going?" he asked.

"Oh, yes . . . the contract negotiations?" I stammered, realizing this was one of the code questions we had agreed to use when communicating with each other inside China. "Well, we had a good negotiation here and everything's OK with our client," I continued awkwardly.

"Glad to hear it," he chirruped. "The contract negotiations here in Hong Kong also went very well, so we'll proceed as planned."

Then there was an awkward pause. I assumed he had gotten a China visa, but having come to the end of our coded script options, neither of us quite knew how to clarify the situation.

"Well, OK, then," I finally said.

"Yeah. OK," he awkwardly repeated. "See you soon."

I was beginning to feel as if I had stepped into a very badly acted cloak-and-dagger film. If Ministry of Public Security eavesdroppers were listening in on our exchange in attempted code, they were surely howling with laughter at our amateurishness!

■ ■ ■

I was awakened once again, this time by an early morning call.

"I need to meet you right away," announced a strident voice without pleasantries. It was Jan Wong from the *Toronto Globe and Mail*, the president of the Beijing Foreign Correspondents Club.

"Is everything alright?" I asked.

"Let's just talk at lunch," she responded peremptorily and gave me a hotel restaurant name.

When I arrived at the designated hotel, she was waiting in the restaurant with James McGregor, the *Wall Street Journal*'s Beijing bureau chief and her successor at the BFCC. Their very somber looks instantly telegraphed that something was wrong.

"Yesterday we received a call from the Sheraton Great Wall Hotel, where your talk was scheduled to be held," began Wong. "The manager informed us that Ministry of Public Security police had appeared at the hotel, ordered him to cancel our event, and . . .

"My event?" I interrupted, suddenly alarmed.

"Yes, they . . . "

"What was the reason?"

"Apparently they didn't like the title of your talk or that you serve on the board of Human Rights Watch."

"Nothing like this has ever happened before, at least during my years here in China," added McGregor, referring to the unprecedented cancellation by security police of a private event organized exclusively for foreign reporters in a room rented in a joint-venture hotel.

Suddenly I was fearful that authorities might have somehow become aware of our *60 Minutes* venture by having their interest piqued in this Beijing Foreign Correspondents Club event. That would put at great risk not only Wu but the CBS crew and me as well. These concerns made me very regretful I had ever agreed to give this talk. My own lack of judgment had put me under scrutiny by the secret police at precisely the moment when I most needed to remain unnoticed.

As I headed back to our hotel, I felt numb. Still, I could not help thinking how self-defeating such punitive actions were for China. They only alienated the very people—in this case, the foreign press corps—the Chinese government otherwise spent so many resources and so much effort trying to cultivate and propagandize. The Chinese expression "To pick up a stone only to drop it on one's own foot" (搬起石头砸自己的脚) seemed apt here. By closing down this private meeting, the Party risked another international incident involving the global media that only made China look more aggressive, autocratic, and retrograde.

Such responses to foreign criticism were, of course, fed by national insecurities and a deep sense of inferiority that had led to repeated cycles in which perceived insults triggered self-defeating counterreactions, which in turn led to further foreign condemnation, followed by a deeper sense of Chinese grievance. The more Chinese leaders felt criticized, scorned, and disrespected by the outside world, the more aggrieved, prideful, defensive, stubborn, and nationalistic they—and many Chinese people—became. It was hardly surprising, then, that China's "Century of Humiliation" (百年国耻), which began at the end of the Qing Dynasty and was then picked up by Chiang Kai-shek in the Nationalist era during the 1930s as the

Japanese began their occupation, kept being recharged with energy by new incidents such as this one. Counterintuitively, they kept happening even during the so-called reform years when China's accrual of "wealth and power" (富强) had actually begun to make impressive advances.

It was just such self-defeating responses to foreign criticisms that led Lu Xun, China's greatest modern writer, to wryly warn nearly a century ago: "Whether we are massacred by our own people, or by foreigners, does not amount to the same thing. For instance, if a man slaps himself, he will not feel insulted, whereas if someone else slaps him, he will feel angry. However, when a man is so far gone that he slaps himself, he fully deserves to be slapped by anyone else who passes by."

The more Chinese leaders "slapped" themselves by doing reprehensible things and then defensively blamed the outside world, the more uncomfortable they became as members of the globalized, cosmopolitan world. Perhaps the most prominent and humiliating instance of recent "self-slapping" was the 1989 Beijing Massacre. By ordering the PLA to wound and kill thousands of its own peacefully demonstrating people, the CCP triggered a massive new cycle of self-humiliation, aggrievement, and then recrimination against the censorious West that had, of course, responded with horrified condemnation.

One of the great promises of the early 2000s was the Party's notion of China striving toward a "peaceful rise" (和平崛起). This was a slogan lofted by none other than the vice principal of the Central Party School, Zheng Bijian, in 2003. It was designed to rebut the "China threat theory" by assuring other countries that China's new wealth and power did not mean it wanted to disrupt the existing global order and world market system, much less harm any other nation or be hegemonic. Suggesting that China might be ready to start vacating its victim culture and instead find a place in the existing world order it had once opposed did, for a while, reassure those who feared that a wealthy and powerful China would mean belligerence, hostility, and disruption.

■ ■ ■

Despite my unnerved state, I decided not to risk upsetting Wu by telling him what had happened to me, much less suggest he delay his trip to Beijing. But the likelihood that I was now under surveillance made it doubly risky for me to plan on doing anything like transporting videotapes out of China or helping him in any way that might endanger him.

My anxieties were hardly allayed when I passed the Palace Hotel's news kiosk and saw that the *International Herald Tribune* had published a front-page article headlined, "China Bars US Scholar's Lecture," reporting on my canceled talk to the Beijing Foreign Correspondents Club.

Such publicity also created another concern. Baifang and I now had to be careful about seeing our own Chinese friends and acquaintances, lest we contaminate them by association with my fallen state of political grace. If they had learned independently about the cancellation of my BFCC talk, I knew many would surely withdraw from further interaction with us. Whenever someone in China gets into political trouble, the almost inevitable consequence is that colleagues, friends, associates, and sometimes even family members start to almost autonomically avoid them out of fear that even peripheral involvement will infect them with political contagion. Such a response is an understandable, if demoralizing, political reality of Chinese life.

When he was arrested during the Anti-Rightist Campaign (1957–1959), Wu was not told what his crimes were. Indeed, he was never sure exactly why he was imprisoned. But I recalled him lamenting how, after his arrest, people began avoiding his family. Being made into a pariah with whom friends, colleagues, and sometimes even family members fear to interact is a far more effective way of making a victim feel culpable than any specific charges or sentence. While a crime can be denied or rebutted, an amorphous accusation of unspecific wrongdoing followed by an official punishment is much harder to repudiate. Instead, it invites the accused to search for the cause of their delinquency within themselves, perhaps even in other wrongdoings of which the indicting authorities are unaware. After all, if there was a punishment, should there not also logically have been a crime? And so, in China, it is often not a crime that presupposes a punishment but a punishment that presupposes a crime. And once punished by the state, victims easily find criminality enough in their own ambiguous hearts to indict themselves in ways that are far more damning and crippling than any formal charge conjured up by the Party or a court.

By nature, I have never been a suspicious person. However, in this newly hostile environment in which I suddenly found myself, I began doubting and mistrusting things that normally would not have attracted my slightest notice.

Was our room phone bugged?

Was the guest next door there to keep us under surveillance?

Who were the two surly looking young men always seated on the hotel lobby couches smoking cigarettes and vacantly staring at us as we passed by?

Was the man lingering over a sandwich in the coffee shop trying to inch closer to listen in on my conversation with Baifang?

When we went out, were we being followed?

In a world so irradiated with distrust, almost anybody seemed a possible adversary and no amount of paranoia seemed excessive.

There was another, even more poisonous dynamic at work: Even though a victim might have done nothing wrong, if accused they could not help feeling somehow responsible for what was happening and then seek blame for their predicament in their own deportment. Paradoxically, as long as one was able to convince oneself that some quotient of blame for whatever had happened was one's own fault, it was still possible to imagine that there could be a self-generated remedy.

▪ ▪ ▪

I had just fallen asleep when our room phone sprang to life.

"Mr. Orville Schell?" said a woman in stern Chinese-accented English.

"Yes."

"This is the hotel reception desk, and you must come down to the lobby immediately."

"Why?"

"To register for your room."

"But my wife already did so several days ago."

"You must register, too."

"Why don't I stop by first thing in the morning?" I suggested as congenially as I could.

"No, you must come now!"

"But . . . "

"It's according to regulations!"

Grudgingly I dressed, assured Baifang I would be right back, and descended to the lobby.

"You did not sign this!" the stony-faced clerk at the reception desk charged, thrusting a blank registration form at me in an accusatory fashion.

"I'm sorry to have inconvenienced you," I responded as politely as I could, sensing I had tripped a wire. "My wife registered before I arrived, so we thought that was adequate."

"Every guest is required to fill out an official registration form," she countered angrily, tapping the blank form with her ballpoint pen. "We must submit these to the relevant authorities" (有关部门). She was, of course, referring to the Ministry of Public Security, which monitored everyone checking in and out of hotels in China.

Dutifully, I filled out the form. But as I rode the elevator back upstairs, I felt chilled. In fact, I was starting to wonder whether I should not just cancel our whole *60 Minutes* plan and immediately go home.

■ ■ ■

The next morning, I was up early for a solitary breakfast. In a matter of hours, Wu and his wife were scheduled to leave

Hong Kong. Because he wanted to avoid the Beijing airport where security was tight, he had decided to fly to Tianjin and then drive to Beijing. If I was going to halt our whole plan, very soon it would be too late.

After agonizing through breakfast, I decided to let things proceed. With all the expense and preparation, it would be a terrible waste and disappointment to scrub the project just because of some inchoate fears. Moreover, I could think of no way of canceling everything that would not leave Wu feeling betrayed.

After all the tension of the past few days, Baifang and I had been looking forward to joining friends for a picnic in the Fragrant Hills outside Beijing. Not wanting to involve these friends unknowingly in our mess, we considered canceling the trip. However, since we would be alone with them and in the countryside, we finally decided we dared go ahead.

Our drive through the blossoming orchards beyond the Summer Palace, with the landscape seeming so tranquil and quotidian, I did feel momentarily released from all the tension that had been building around us. Along the narrow country road, we passed peasants in their fields, mule carts on the shoulder, and birds chirping, all of which made things seem blessedly normal. As we sat with our friends on a hillside and ate lunch together, fears that someone might have been tailing us evaporated. I was in no hurry to break the spell.

Alas, all too soon it was time to return. And as we drew ever nearer Beijing, I felt as if we were approaching closer and closer to a red-hot stove.

Chapter Ten

THE GREAT WITHIN

WU AND HIS WIFE were scheduled to land in Tianjin at midday, and if nothing unexpected happened, they had promised to call. I waited nervously, checking my watch every few minutes.

Finally, the phone rang.

"This is Peter," an excited voice announced. "The first stage of our contract has gone through without a problem!"

"Well . . . good! Did you get any nice samples?" I asked, groping for our coded way of inquiring about how he was feeling about his trip.

"What?" asked Wu, uncertain how to reply. I realized that our codes for in-China communications made no provision for expressing feelings of relief.

"No! I mean, did you have good luck getting the samples through customs?" I asked, trying to learn whether he had had any trouble at customs himself.

"Oh, no!" he replied, suddenly understanding. "No problems, and we'll arrive at our next stop tomorrow."

"Oh, OK," I stammered, wishing he had not been quite so explicit. Since he was still unaware of my delicate situation, the last thing I wanted him to do was reach out directly when he got to our hotel in Beijing. However, I was not sure how to convey that prohibition. "Peter, we've had some problems with our negotiations here," I finally said, trying to sound as matter-of-fact as possible.

"OK, but we'll be coming on anyway," he replied, not understanding what I was trying to convey.

"Negotiations here have . . . " I began. "Well, we've run into some complications," I continued more forcefully. Then, fearful I had been too alarmist, I added, "But I think things will be alright for your trip." Then, wanting to terminate this confusing interaction, I said, "So, good luck."

"Well, OK," he replied. There was an unmistakable tremor of uncertainty in his voice as he hung up.

Before coming on to Beijing, Wu had planned to hire a private car in Tianjin and try to drive with his wife out into the Qinghe Prison camp, a massive agricultural complex of fields that were not all surrounded by walls and fences, and just see if they were stopped. He planned to use the pretext of seeking out an old friend who, since his release, had become a prison guard. As I thought about his plan, I began to wonder what I would do if anything happened to him there? How would I even find out? And if I did learn of trouble, what would I actually be able to do to help him?

▪ ▪ ▪

While Baifang and I were at lunch in a private room at a joint-venture hotel restaurant with a friend who was the daughter of a former high-ranking Chinese leader, she confided that she had heard about the cancellation of the BFCC event. But it was only when I told her that she realized the incident involved me. When I asked if she knew who ordered the cancellation, she pointed wordlessly toward the ceiling.

"If you had gone, you would have been detained."

After delivering this upsetting news, she said she would not have come to lunch had she known I was the one involved. And then, because she now wanted to avoid being spotted with us, she asked if we would both stay seated while she departed.

As we watched her go, I felt more dispirited than ever. Not only had I put our *60 Minutes* effort in jeopardy, but now I had started endangering friends as well.

Later that same afternoon, Baifang told me that two other Chinese friends who had invited us for dinner that night were suddenly "too busy" to see us. While I understood the ineluctable logic of why, this cancellation was nonetheless unnerving. Precisely when we would have appreciated the company of friends, we were becoming untouchable.

What was happening was a testament to the power of the unique kind of social ostracization and psychological isolation that the Chinese state and party are capable of mustering against individuals it wishes to target. If it could throw U.S. citizens with American passports like us off balance with just a few turns of the screw, what would it feel like to be a Chinese unable to escape back to another life abroad? The growing sense of quarantine and isolation that had started to envelope us offered only a hint of the extreme duress a Chinese would experience in the same situation.

■ ■ ■

Back at our hotel, a cryptic voicemail awaited:

"Contact the reception desk regarding urgent message."

When I again presented myself at the front desk, a clerk passed me a folded, handwritten note: "Contact Director Men Bo, the Beijing Public Security Bureau's Department of Foreign Affairs on Beichizi at 2:30 p.m."

My heart sank. We had been summoned to the local branch of the Ministry of Public Security (PSB), China's much feared domestic police and security agency. Anticipating the worst, I gathered up our address books and my notepads and put them in our hotel safe, just in case our room was searched while we were gone. The last thing I wanted was for the PSB to gain access to the contacts for all our friends, many of whom were writers, filmmakers, and intellectuals with political problems of their own.

Unable to quite believe what was unfolding, a few hours later Baifang and I took a pedicab down Goldfish Alley (金鱼胡同) to the Public Security Bureau branch office on Beichizi (北池子), just across the canal around the Forbidden City. All the way, I worried that all this drama would have an impact on our unborn child. Then suddenly we were standing in front of the compound housing the Foreign Affairs Department of the local PSB. We rang and waited anxiously while the gatekeeper announced us to the "great within" (大内), as the interior of the Forbidden City was known during imperial times.

Soon, two crisply uniformed police officers appeared.

"You are to be questioned in different rooms," one sternly announced in wooden English.

"Are you Director Men Bo?" I asked.

"No," he replied icily. "You will be taken to separate rooms."

"I'm sorry, but we will not be separated," I remonstrated as calmly as I could.

"According to our internal regulations, you will be questioned in separate rooms," he repeated.

"Where is Director Men?" My interlocutor pointed to the man beside him. "Why have we been summoned here?" I asked Men directly. From the opaque look on his face, it was evident he did not understand English well.

"This you will learn later," answered Men's colleague.

"I'd like an answer now," I persisted.

"You must go to separate rooms for questioning," barked Men himself, speaking directly to Baifang in Chinese.

"My wife is pregnant, and we will not be separated," I reiterated. "If you wish to charge us with some wrongdoing, let us know what we've done. If we're going to have a friendly conversation, we must be in the same room," I continued, using a Chinese euphemism.

"This is not a 'friendly conversation,' " Men's cohort shot back. "This is an investigation."

"An investigation of what?"

Just then a thundershower arrived, speckling the carefully pressed uniforms of the two policemen with raindrops. We were hurried across the courtyard to a room that, like most official meeting halls in China, centered around a U-shaped arrangement of elephantine stuffed chairs adorned with white lace antimacassars on each arm. A lone traditional Chinese landscape painting hung forlornly on one wall.

After several more police officers had seated themselves against the walls, Men sat down on a thronelike chair facing us as if he were a judge. On a lower level sat a woman taking notes.

"Show me your passports," Men asked peremptorily. I handed both documents to a dour-looking police officer, who began leafing through them. Since they were critical to leaving China, I immediately regretted having relinquished them. "When did you enter the People's Republic of China?" demanded Men.

"June 5th."

"What kind of passport do you have?

"What's your profession?

"How old are you?

"Why did you come to China?

"Where did you get your visa?"

The relentlessness of his questioning was hypnotic. Men's colleagues stared at us with impassive blankness, leaving me wondering how many hundreds of such interrogations they had attended.

"Did you register at the hotel when you came in?"

"Not when I came in."

"When did you, in fact, register?"

"On June 8th, when I was summoned to the reception desk after I was already asleep."

Was this my transgression, I wondered? Or did they know more and were just baiting some kind of a trap?

"So, you arrived on June 5th, but it was not until June 8th that you actually registered?" continued Men accusatorially. Then, he plucked up my hotel registration form from a side table and waved it as if it was a piece of incriminating evidence at a trial.

"This was not an intentional act," I said. "It never occurred to me that both members of a married couple must register, and . . . "

"But, did you register upon arriving?" repeated Men. "Just answer the question, yes or no! Our computer link with the hotel will tell us the truth." Men glanced down at the notes his scribe was furiously scribbling.

"My failure to fill out this form was not a purposeful act," I repeated. "Elsewhere it's quite adequate for one member of a couple alone to register at a hotel."

"So, you admit your error?" smiled Men triumphantly.

"I . . . "

"Did you, or did you not, violate the regulations of the People's Republic of China by entering one of our hotels without registering?" he interrupted.

"I didn't know that there were such regulations."

"Is it not the responsibility of foreign guests to know the rules and regulations of the host countries they visit?" Since I had no argument for such a challenge, I just nodded. "So, you admit you're wrong," persisted Men.

"I admit to registering several days after arriving in Beijing, because I assumed my wife's registration was adequate for a married couple sharing one room," I wearily rejoined.

"So, you do admit your error," repeated Men, displeased with the caveats in my confession.

"That's for you to determine," I replied.

"You realize this is a very serious matter," he countered.

"Requiring guests to register at a hotel is an internationally recognized sovereign right, so you have violated Chinese law." He pulled out a pamphlet entitled "The Laws of the People's Republic of China on Entry and Exit of Aliens," opened it, and began reading as if from scripture.

"I admit to registering a few days after I arrived in Beijing and apologize for my error," I said, trying to find some common ground. "But what's the real reason you've summoned us here?"

"Now that you understand our rules and regulations, perhaps you will not make such mistakes again," replied Men with a preemptive air of finality. In the time-honored fashion of seasoned interrogators who often seek a last-minute note of good cheer before allowing a victim to leave, Men gave an unconvincing smile. "We just needed a thorough investigation to clear up this matter. Whether it was intentional or not, you broke the law. But now that you've confessed, you must pay a fine before you go."

"A fine?" I yelped. Then it occurred to me that this might be a face-saving way of ending the matter, a kind of Chinese Communist nolo contendere plea option that would allow the interrogation to conclude and us to leave. "Please tell me how much," I offered, reaching obligingly for my wallet. "I'd like to pay and take my wife back to our hotel!"

"No!" said Men raising an admonishing hand like a traffic cop. "We must look into this matter further before a final judgement is delivered."

The sour-faced police officer who had been studying our passports strode officiously over to Men and whispered something in his ear. The two examined my passport together for several minutes. Then the sour-faced officer spun around and, holding my passport open to the page on which my most recent visa had been stamped, charged: "You've altered your visa to China!"

Dumbfounded, I asked to see what he was referring to. When he showed me the offending part of the visa, the only possible "alteration" I could detect was that the vermillion ink on one letter of the visa stamp was a little blurred."

"This could only be the result of something that your government's own officials did when stamping my visa," I protested, not wanting to become the butt of a trumped-up visa forgery charge. As I remonstrated, the sour-faced officer started walking toward the back door with our passports. "I'm sorry," I cried out and jumped up to stop him. "Please do not take our personal property from this room!"

What panicked me was the thought that once our passports left the room, they might not reappear, making it impossible for us to leave the country. What is more, if our passports left our sight, someone could actually make alterations to the visas in order to justify their claims that I had tampered with the stamp. As I reached out, the policeman angrily jerked the passports away.

"We must have experts examine your visa further," he snarled, slapping the cover of my passport with the back of his hand. "Why are you so afraid?" he taunted. "Do you think we'd take your passport?"

Then a female police officer entered the room, studied the visa for a few moments, turned authoritatively to Men, and murmured, "No problem."

Grudgingly, the now even more sour-faced policeman handed back my passport. Then, just as I hoped we would be dismissed, a second officer changed places with Men and started the interrogation again, this time in Chinese with Baifang.

'What's your full name?"

"Where were you born?"

"When did you leave China?"

"Why did you leave your homeland?"

"What's your profession?"

"When did you come back?"

"Why are you here?"

The gazes of all the other police officials facing us had suddenly swiveled from me to Baifang, who sat glumly, barely able to contain her indignation.

"There's only one question," her glowering interrogator demanded.

"Do you admit to having violated Chinese regulations?"

"You're just searching for bones in an egg!" (鸡蛋里挑骨头), she countered in Chinese.

While I was a foreigner who might expect to be excused from certain procedural errors, even of certain mutinous tendencies, as a Chinese from right here in Beijing, Baifang was afforded no such latitude. Because of her heritage, she was considered an irrevocable part of ethnic China and thus someone from whom such remonstration was considered treasonous. She began to cry, and all I wanted was to levitate her out of this upsetting charade as quickly as possible.

"My wife has done nothing wrong!" I interjected angrily. "If I have inadvertently failed to obey some regulations, please forgive me, but do not blame her. And be assured that it was not either of our intentions to do anything wrong."

As I said this, I was feeling somewhat disingenuous, because I was, of course, painfully aware of the myriad close associations we had both had over the years with dissident Chinese intellectuals and artists. While there is nothing illegal about such friendships, I knew that the Public Security Bureau had dossiers stuffed with materials about me and looked on such associations as the equivalent of consorting with the enemy. And then there were all the critical writings on China I had penned over the decades. This was certainly part of my record that, from their point of view, made me someone who had shown a less than adequate demonstrations of "friendship."

"As a Chinese, don't you feel any guilt for not reminding your foreign husband to register according to law?" the interrogator asked.

"No!" Baifang riposted. "We are separate people!"

"For whom do you work?"

"It's not relevant." She was angry now.

"Why have you come back to China?"

"To see my parents."

Her interrogation droned on for another exhausting hour. When it finally ended, the woman who had been scribbling notes rose and handed us each a "transcript" written in very cursive Chinese that was impossible for me to read.

"In accordance with our regulations, you will sign these," ordered Men, receiving some papers from his scribe.

"Can I get a translation?" I asked.

"No," he shot back.

"Can we get a copy?"

"No."

"Can we copy the document ourselves?"

After some whispered deliberation, they consented to allow us to hand copy it, even though it would take hours to compete. But then Baifang leaned over and whispered that her stomach had begun to hurt, and I could tell she was at the end of her tether. Nor was I in any mood to continue resisting. How quickly such experiences enervate and undermine one's sense of righteousness and erode one's powers of resistance! Maybe that was precisely the function of such interrogations: Just wear down victims until they confess to anything. Anyway, by that time, all I wanted was to be released. So, finally we signed the transcript. However, beside my name I scrawled in English: "This is only a rough precis of our PSB interrogation on June 10, 1991."

"Now you may go," said Men. "However, for the next few days you must stay by your phone and in Beijing."

We had just collapsed on our bed back in our hotel room, when the phone rang. Wearily I answered.

"Hello, this is Peter." It was Wu's familiar voice sounding unexpectedly cheerful. "The contract in Tianjin has been signed most excellently, everything else went well, and we'll be arriving tomorrow."

We had been so preoccupied with our interrogation and other things that I had hardly had a chance to even think about Wu's arrival in Tianjin or whether his trip to the Qinghe Farm had worked out. But our hackneyed coded conversation suggested he had not only arrived but been successful in getting into his old camp.

"Well," I replied haltingly. "We're having some problems with our negotiations at this end, and . . . "

"I hope it's not serious," he replied hopefully. "We'll be checking into the Palace Hotel soon." Then he hung up.

At least he was alright. However, the imminence of his arrival made it imperative that I somehow find a way to alert him to my situation. The last thing I wanted him to do was try to make direct contact once he arrived. Truth be told, I was so rattled I was again wondering whether Baifang and I should not just head to the airport and leave China before something irrevocable happened.

But then . . . who would accept the first tranche of tapes Wu might have shot in Qinghe? And who would pick up the second tranche when he returned from the coal mines in Shanxi Province? Finally, who would provide backup when Wu moved on to Shanghai?

If I stayed, I knew I needed a way of giving Wu a heads-up about what had been happening so he could make up his own mind about how dangerous the situation was and how he could best protect himself and his wife. But since I was almost certainly being shadowed, how could we safely communicate?

Then an idea suddenly occurred to me.

I had a friend, John Krich, who worked for the *Wall Street Journal* in Southeast Asia and had just arrived in Beijing for a visit. Since he was staying at another hotel, he would be a perfect neutral party to leave a note for Wu's wife at the Palace Hotel reception desk asking her to meet him for coffee. Then, face-to-face, he could let her know what had been happening so they could make their own decision about how to proceed.

■ ■ ■

At 6:00 a.m., as I was headed to the hotel coffee shop for breakfast with Krich, I noticed a copy of the *People's Daily* on the news rack outside the restaurant that carried a front-page column headlined "The Tree Wishes to Remain Calm, But the Wind Will Not Allow It," attacking the foreign media for how it had been covering the anniversary of the Beijing Massacre. It accused foreign journalists of being "hostile foreign forces (境外敌对势力) harboring hatred" for China and just "waiting for some kind of sensational major news" in order to "change the choice and the will of the Chinese people," who, the columnist said, were resolutely set on continuing down the road of "socialism with Chinese characteristics" (中国特色社会主义). Having effectively stifled their own domestic press, Party leaders found it increasingly intolerable that foreign correspondents were still able not only to freely criticize China's one-party rule and its human rights abuses but to do so right from Chinese soil.

Wearily, I sat down in the restaurant to compose a note that Krich could pass on to Wu's wife, Chen Ching-li. My challenge was to write something into which I could insert "My hands are on both of my ears," a code Wu had used while he was under detention to signal other political detainees to stay away from him. Then I added: "I think things will be OK for your own negotiations." Finally, I signed the note using my code name, "Jonathan."

When Krich arrived, it was a welcome relief to be with someone not involved in politics. He was in Beijing courting a woman with whom he had become smitten on a previous trip. Listening to his problems with his elusive Chinese paramour provided a soothing distraction from all our political travails. However, as I was sliding the envelope with my note for Wu's wife across the table to him, I noticed that the coffee shop was equipped with two security cameras that were rotating robotically around, scanning the room. They brought me back to the reality of where we were and this project's many dangers.

■ ■ ■

Although I had decided not to openly contact most of my foreign journalist friends in Beijing, lest my already delicate situation be made even more precarious, I did want to be in touch with a few in case Wu ended up in trouble and I needed to get some quick media attention. One of them was Katherine Wilhelm, Associated Press's Beijing bureau chief.

"The situation has been pretty bad during the last few months," she told me when we met at a hotel restaurant for lunch. "I've been followed a lot, and we all assume our phones are bugged. Of course, we also know that our Chinese employees, all of whom are assigned to us by the government-run Foreign Enterprises Human Resources Service Co. (FESCO), are informants. With the PSB intimidating so many of our Chinese sources, few dare talk to us. And because we don't want to get them in trouble, our ability to use even what they're willing to say is also limited. That prevents us from doing a good job of reporting,"

"Were you followed here to lunch today?" I asked, trying not to sound too suspicious.

"I don't think so, which surprises me," she answered with an uncertain smile. "But you never know. Sometimes they'll follow us very obviously for a while, and then they stop. Their logic is hard to figure out. I think they often just want to intimidate us."

When Wilhelm left, I watched as she walked out through the hotel lobby. No sooner had she reached the main door than one of the young Chinese men who had been lounging on a lobby couch stood up, stubbed out his cigarette, and stalked her out the door, albeit, at a discreet distance. As she turned onto the sidewalk, he stopped between two parked cars and raised a small black case to his mouth. Watching this well-choreographed ballet of surveillance was a reminder that I too needed to be more attentive to whether I was being tailed.

As I crossed the hotel lobby, I noticed several other young Chinese men on couches also clutching black leatherette cases.

So, as soon as I passed through the revolving front door, I stopped and, as if I had forgotten something inside, went back through the door the other way. Just as I did, one of the young men who had been lounging on the couches was coming out the other way. When he saw me through the glass door panel going in the opposite direction, he did an almost cartoonlike double take.

Since I had no way of knowing whether Wu had received my note via Krich or even if he had arrived safely at the Palace Hotel, when I finally arrived back in our hotel lobby I slipped into the alcove where the house phones were located. When an operator picked up, I asked her to connect me with the room of Chen Ching-li, Wu's Taiwan-born wife. As soon as the line started ringing, I hung up. Now at least I knew they had arrived and checked in.

■ ■ ■

On past trips to China, I had been largely oblivious of the growing number of surveillance systems. But now that I was becoming attuned to them, I was seeing a PSB presence everywhere. So, the next afternoon Baifang and I decide to take a harmless stroll just to see what would happen.

As we headed out into the hot, smoggy day, a young man with curly hair, dark glasses, and a telltale walkie-talkie case in hand rose from one of the hotel lobby couches and fell in behind us.

No sooner had we crossed the intersection of Gold Fish Alley and Wangfujing than another young man in regimental sunglasses who was standing on the corner raised his own telltale black case to his ear and fell in with our tail.

The ubiquity of these agents triggered an almost pheromonic chemical reaction within me. Like a fox being chased by hounds, I was overcome by an uncontrollable impulse to somehow outwit our pursuers. I was, of course, afraid. However, the other animal part that was almost autonomically programmed for escape also kicked in to try to reverse the prey-versus-predator relationship.

Baifang and I were halfway down Nanchizi (南池子) when an empty cab came by, and I impulsively flagged it down. We piled in. But, in just two blocks, a red motorcycle with two helmeted riders fell in behind us and tailed our cab through Tiananmen Square, followed us past the stony visage of Chairman Mao hanging on the Gate of Heavenly Peace, and then turned left to follow us past the Great Hall of the People. The scenes of tourists strolling through the great square, taking snapshots, and enjoying themselves made things looks so ordinary and pacific, it was hard to believe that just two years ago this very place had roiled with hundreds of thousands of smiling, banner-toting, chanting, protesting demonstrators optimistically marching for democracy and greater openness.

I had asked our driver to take us to Liulichang (琉璃厂), an ancient alley lined with book stores and art galleries, and all the way the motorcycle stayed behind us like a skiff being towed by a larger boat. When we arrived there, as I was paying the driver, I noticed not only that the motor bike had stopped just behind us, but that the riders had been met by three colleagues.

Not sure what else to do, Baifang and I got out of the cab and entered one of the art galleries, from where I was able to study our two new tails through a window. One was attired in a drip-dry, short-sleeved white shirt, perma-pressed slacks, and dark sunglasses. The other was incongruously dressed in a sleeveless tank top, shorts, and sockless, high-heeled plastic sandals, a mutant form of footwear that was then a male fashion statement in Beijing.

When we ducked into another shop that sold books and stone rubbings, one of our tails, perhaps worried we might sneak out a back door, followed us inside, sat down on a bench, yawned, and lit a cigarette. Seeing this fellow in such mortal closeness somehow emboldened me. Hoping to transform myself from the hunted into the hunter, I sidled over to him.

"Hi! How are you doing?" I said, greeting him in Chinese. My quarry blinked like a wild creature awakened in his burrow in the middle of the night by a bright light. "So, you must be interested in art and literature," I continued, gesturing at all the books and stone rubbings arrayed around us.

"Uh-huh," he stammered uncomfortably.

"Maybe we can become friends!" I declared with saccharine enthusiasm, using a phrase that Chinese youths commonly used (我们可以做好朋友) when approaching foreigners in public parks in the hope of finding a partner with whom they could practice their English. "Tell me, what kinds of books interest you?"

"Oh, umm . . . Well, actually I prefer history," he haltingly replied, clearly made uneasy by this unscheduled assignation.

"What luck!" I effused. "I happen to be interested in history, too! Tell me, what historical periods do you enjoy most?"

"Well . . . new stuff," he responded, eyes darting, perhaps hoping one of his other comrades would come to his rescue.

"Oh, I love modern history, too," I crooned.

"Uh . . . ," he grunted.

"Yes, in fact, sometimes I write essays on modern Chinese history, you know, on politics, student demonstrations, prisons, massacres, etc.," I deadpanned. When he did not respond, I ventured, "Maybe we could get together sometime and talk more." He looked at me with wild-eyed uneasiness. Baifang was by now glowering at me as if I had lost my senses.

"I have to go now," my new "friend" suddenly ejaculated and unceremoniously exited the shop.

My spirits had been somehow uplifted by this symbolic, if absurd, counteroffensive against our pursuers. It had for the moment turned the psychology and left me feeling less helpless.

Baifang pulled me out of the bookstore, and we scuttled down Liulichang into one of the most ancient parts of Beijing, where networks of narrow, twisting alleys, or *hutong* (胡同), crisscrossed the neighborhood like a maze of tiny capillaries. But when I glanced back, I saw our tails were still in hot pursuit.

As we approached a junction where one *hutong* intersected another and the line of sight between us and our tails was momentarily obscured, I impulsively pulled her into the smaller alley and we tried to pick up our pace. But it was mercilessly hot under the broiling sun, and Baifang looked very uncomfortable. When a few moments later I looked behind us again, I did not see anyone following.

When we emerged onto Xuanwumen (宣武门), I hailed a cab.

However, my sense of triumph was short-lived. For in China there is no ultimate escape from the state's watchful eye.

That night, we had been invited to attend a friend's birthday party. Because our unexplained absence might be taken as a slight, we decided to go for a short time despite our predicament. But, as soon as we left the hotel, we realized we had made the wrong decision. We were again followed and, not wanting to put our friends in jeopardy, we turned back to the hotel.

We were trapped in a ghoulish paradox, one that was all too familiar to Chinese. Once a person became victimized by some kind of public accusations of political wrongdoing, he or she cryptically became both the destroyed and the destroyer. Being accused, followed, put under surveillance, and possibly even detained was to be anointed into victimhood. But at the same time, the victim was also endowed with new, if unwelcomed, destructive powers, the ability to politically harm others through simple association. So, victims of political harassment and persecution unwillingly became victims and victimizers simultaneously. In one deft stroke, the Party was able to create a devastating double bind: First, its political attacks against its real or imagined enemies rendered them untouchable. Second, it was able to imbue its victims with an involuntary but immensely destructive power to harm others, especially those who were closest to them. Cast into such a double jeopardy, a victim hardly needed physical restraint. Crippled by accusation and turned into a menace at the same time, a person was twice victimized and put into such a state of psychological self-doubt they often became almost completely paralyzed.

China might not have produced a Sigmund Freud to assist the Party in understanding how human psychology worked, but in some deeply instinctual way its leaders had intuited how to inculcate sufficient amounts of guilt, culpability, and self-loathing into their critics' psyches to neutralize them in ways that not even prison officials could accomplish. After all, what human being wants their own travails, whether deserved or not, to also become a source of harm for their friends and loved ones?

■ ■ ■

As I waited in the hotel lobby the next morning, a phalanx of camera-laden French tourists poured out of the elevator bank and surged toward a fleet of buses outside. Then, suddenly, there he was! Wu was striding across the lobby behind the Frenchmen, with Ching-li by his side, heading right toward the couches where the tails were seated. He was wearing a short-sleeved, open-necked sports shirt and had a camera bag slung jauntily over one shoulder, so that he looked like any other tourist headed for the Great Wall.

My first impulse was to spring to my feet and greet him. However, I caught myself, just as he noticed me. I could see that he too had a difficult time restraining himself. It was not until he had almost passed that he reached up and touched both of his earlobes, signaling me he had gotten my note. I quickly touched my own earlobes. He gave a suggestion of a nod, then was gone. Fortunately, as he passed the couches where the tails were perched like crows on a phone wire, no one rose to follow him.

It was a relief to know that he and Ching-li were here and seemingly unburdened by the vagaries of my own situation. If he had gotten any intimation that he was under observation, I am certain Wu would have immediately left the hotel, sent his wife out of the country, and vanished underground. I knew he had brought with him his original Chinese identity card and even an old faded Mao jacket, just in case he needed to suddenly blend in.

The plan for that day called for them to try to penetrate Tuanhe Farm (Beijing No.1 Reform-Through-Labor Detachment), an agricultural camp not far from Beijing where, during the 1960s, he had spent four years working in vegetable fields and brick kilns and had also been locked in solitary confinement for a long period of time.

▪ ▪ ▪

Because Baifang and I had decided it was too dangerous for either of us to try to carry videotapes out of the country, we called up James Husky, an American official we knew who covered Chinese politics at the U.S. Embassy. He was one of the few U.S. diplomats remaining at the embassy who had been present on the night of June 4, 1989, when PLA soldiers fired on protesters in the Beijing Massacre.

When we met at his diplomatic compound apartment, I did not tell him exactly what we were up to. However, since in the past we had talked about human rights problems and political imprisonment, he had a good sense that I was not just vacationing in China. After we finished chatting, he accompanied me down in the elevator and, as we approached the guards at the gate, he leaned over and whispered, "If there's ever anything you need to get out of the country in our diplomatic pouch from the embassy, please know you can count on me."

He seemed to have intuited everything I wanted to convey without my having to say a word. His intelligence and generosity filled me with a profound sense of gratitude.

"Thanks," I said warmly. "Someday I'll explain."

He winked knowingly.

■ ■ ■

When I told Baifang about Husky's offer, she was relieved. However, she still insisted that after we got the tapes off to the embassy, we needed to leave China. So, we headed immediately over to the United Airlines office to change our tickets. With its familiar blue, orange, white, and red logo emblazoned on the front of the counter and its poster of the Statue of Liberty looking out from one of the walls in the sitting area, the office was strangely reassuring. It reminded me that, come what may, Baifang and I, unlike our Chinese compatriots, could always leave China and go home.

As we were waiting for the United Airlines agent to become free, it hit me: This was the perfect rendezvous and drop-off spot for Wu and me! It was a public space where we both had cause to be, and it was located on the second floor of a high-rise building that was not visible from the street. What is more, being neither a Chinese state-owned enterprise nor a joint-venture company, there were no Chinese security guards at the door. So, after changing our plane reservations, I asked the ticket agent if I could use her phone. Then I called the Palace Hotel and left a message for Wu's wife: "United Airlines requests you drop by the ticket office to meet with Jonathan tomorrow morning at 9:00 a.m."

I hoped that if anyone was scanning Wu's messages, they would simply dismiss this one as an anodyne communication from an airline. Then I told the United agent I would return for our reissued tickets first thing the next morning.

■ ■ ■

The closer I got to the United Airlines office the following morning, the more apprehensive I became. While I knew Wu's general plans, I had no idea if he had been able to shoot any video at Qinghe or run into any kind of trouble since arriving. What if he failed to show up? How would I get him the large envelope containing a stack of new videocassettes, the $1,800 in cash we wanted him to have in case he needed it, and the note I had written letting him know that Baifang and I planned to return home the day after tomorrow?

As I entered the airline office, I was stunned to see that Wu and Ching-li were already there in the waiting room. They seemed almost chimerical! The ticket office was otherwise empty, and the agent was primping her hair behind the counter, taking no notice of us. Seeing no surveillance cameras, I walked over to where they were seated on a leatherette banquet, sat down beside Wu, but did nothing more than nod discreetly in his direction, as one might do to any stranger with whom one is sharing a bench in a public place. Then, as nonchalantly as possible, I place my packet of videocassettes and money between us on the banquette. Next, I put my leather shoulder bag down beside it and opened the flap. With no prompting, Wu dropped a large envelope inside and took my packet.

"Tape?" he asked in a whisper.

"Yes. How are you?"

"We had trouble," he said sotto voce, his jaw clenching. "Stopped by guards at Tuanhe. Had to throw away one camera."

"Still have the other?"

"Yes.

"You both OK?"

"OK, but it was close. Leaving today on the train for Taiyuan and Shanxi coal mines."

"OK. We leave day after tomorrow for home. PSB is all over me, but don't think they've made any connection between us." Wu nodded. "When you've gotten into a few camps, get out!" I counseled. "No more risk than necessary. OK?"

He nodded and gave my arm a reassuring squeeze. Suddenly all the anxiety, uncertainty, and stress of the past few months seemed worthwhile.

"Can I help you?" the United ticket agent suddenly piped up.

"Oh yes," I replied, coming back to my senses. "I'm here to pick up some reissued tickets."

I was relieved to have some legitimate business there, because I still needed to use United's phone to call Husky and arrange a drop-off for Wu's tapes. As I dialed his number, my hand was trembling.

"Hi!" Husky's wife, Joanne, answered.

"You'll probably recognize me by the sound of my voice," I told her, not wanting to say my name, because the phones of all Western diplomats in China were known to be bugged.

"Oh yes," she responded. "You're the one with the brightly colored necktie."

"Just so," I replied, glad she was being discreet and simply recalling the colorful tie I had worn when we last had dinner.

"May I stop by in a little while?"

"My husband's out, but come by anyway."

As I took a taxi to their diplomatic compound, the videocassettes in my briefcase felt almost radioactive. At their building, the elevator operator was one of those women in all compounds assigned to foreigners whose real function was not to run the elevator but to watch and record who comes and goes. But her look of infinite boredom made her look reassuringly unconcerned about me. Nonetheless, after exiting the elevator, I waited until the doors had fully closed behind me before walking to the Husky's apartment door.

When Joanne Husky opened the door, I asked her to forgive my abruptness, but for obvious reasons I did not want to linger.

"This is just something for the diplomatic pouch, and here's the address to which it should be sent," I said.

"Don't worry," she said smiling. "We know what to do and are glad to help."

"My thanks to both of you" was all I said.

■ ■ ■

On our last day in Beijing, I lunched with the BBC's James Miles and the (London) *Times*'s Catherine Sampson. I asked them how they viewed the post-1989 strength of the Chinese government.

"Well, that's the question of questions, isn't it?" responded Miles, shaking his head. "It could be gone tomorrow or linger on for years. One can equally imagine either scenario."

Miles's comment was a reminder that, despite what had happened to the USSR and Eastern Europe after 1989, the Chinese Communist Party was not necessarily breathing its last. Communism may have vanished elsewhere around the globe, but it was hanging on in Asia, not just in China but in North Korea, Vietnam, and Laos as well.

■ ■ ■

Baifang and I left for San Francisco just as Wu and his wife were heading to China's northwest Shanxi Province and coal country. As we winged our way toward Japan watching a Hollywood movie, it was difficult to imagine Wu in the Wangzhuang Coal Mine (Shanxi No. 4 Reform-Through-Labor

Detachment), where he had spent nine years; the Guozhuang Coal Mine (Shanxi No. 13 Reform-Through-Labor Detachment); or the Yinying Coal Mine (Shanxi No. 2 Reform-Through-Labor Detachment), where he had spent several more years as a "forced job placement" worker after his formal sentence ended.

When we initially discussed his current plan, Wu had insisted it would be relatively easy for him to penetrate these mines because other "forced job placement" personnel he once knew were still working there. His plan was simply to show up with his new wife, pretend they were on a sentimental visit, and then informally shoot some video as he showed her around the mines where he had once worked.

After that, his plan called for them to go on to Shanghai so he could show her where he had grown up. But while there, he also hoped to get into an urban prison factory that manufactured hand tools by pretending to be an overseas Chinese businessman from the United States interested in placing a large order.

Chapter Eleven

HOMECOMING

SEVERAL DAYS after we landed back in San Francisco, Wu's tapes arrived via the U.S. Embassy diplomatic pouch. Gelber was ecstatic. But when I suggested I might take a quick look at them, he urged me to wait.

"We really need Wu to guide us through what he's shot so we'll know what we're looking at and what the circumstance of each shoot was," he said. "As soon as he gets back, Doug and I will fly out to the West Coast and we'll all screen them together."

■ ■ ■

To my great relief, a week later Wu arrived back safely in San Francisco. However, he reported, the last leg of his journey had not been without drama.

"Just as we were leaving Shanghai, the guy I'd lined up to take the second batch of tapes and documents out of the country for us canceled," he told me when we had a chance to talk. "So, Ching-li and I had to rush from Shanghai to Hangzhou, where I had a friend working at the airport who helped me get the stuff safely through customs inspection. But still, Ching-li had to hide some of the documents we got in her underwear! I can't tell you how relieved we were when our plane finally left that runway for Hong Kong!"

Now that he was out of China, there seemed to be a new air of confidence, even a little bravado, in his voice.

"When I let Hewitt know that Wu had gotten into a few camps, had managed to shoot some footage, and was now out of China, he was incredibly excited!" effused Gelber as we talked on the phone the next day. "Doug and I have booked tickets for tomorrow to San Francisco. After we get there, we'll all sit down together and see what we've got."

■ ■ ■

Since returning from China, I had been trying to visualize the camps, farms, mines, factories, and prisons that Wu was revisiting. On one of his calls, he had regaled me with how, posing as an overseas Chinese American businessman, he had gotten into two Shanghai reform-through-labor prison factories, the Laodong Steel Pipe Factory and the Huadong Electrical Welding Factory. At the first factory, he had even managed to pocket two documents that officials had carelessly left out on a table. One was a map showing the locations and names of all the other prisons in Shanghai. The other was a written report on how to suppress prison escapes and riots. But more importantly, it sounded as though he had gotten enough tape and material for a good television story.

■ ■ ■

Gelber and Hamilton arrived in California the next morning. After they checked into the grand old Claremont Hotel in Berkeley, we all assembled around a huge TV monitor in Gelber's suite. Everyone was on edge with anticipation. As the first videocassette slid into the player, a hush fell over the room. We watched as Wu appeared on the screen walking through Tianjin Airport, looking like any other overseas Chinese tourist arriving back in "The Motherland" (祖国) for a nostalgic visit.

Sensing our surprise at this banal opening sequence, Wu explained he had purposely shot these innocuous initial scenes so that if authorities ever seized his tapes, they might be dissuaded from watching further by such a seemingly innocent initial sequence of homecoming.

Next came several disjointed minutes of bicycle riders and traffic on a dusty, gray Tianjin street. Then the screen erupted in a burst of green as the camera panned out over a vast, flat field.

"That's it!" said Wu, jumping up.

"That's what?" asked Gelber.

"That's the Qinghe Farm," Wu replied with enormous excitement.

"One of the places you were imprisoned?" asked Gelber.

"Yeah, twice and for more than four years! It's a huge agricultural complex of marshland reclaimed for agriculture by prisoners like me. And it's still managed by the Beijing Municipal Government."

Then the camera began jerking around before finally focusing on a brick wall surrounding a nondescript building.

"OK!" said Wu, jumping up again. "Those are the walls of one of the prison compounds at Qinghe! See, there's a guard tower! And, look! There's some barbed wire!"

For a fleeting instant, we caught sight of a brick tower and a wall garlanded with razor wire. But just as quickly as the camera had focused on the wire, it started to wobble, and the screen dissolved back into a blur of gray sky.

As Gelber punched in the next cassette, everyone waited with silent expectation.

"What's that?" asked Gelber, his voice tinged with anxiety as two gateposts affixed with signs in Chinese flickered on the screen.

"That's the entrance to one of the Qinghe Farm's reform-through-labor detachments," responded Wu excitedly. But no sooner had he spoken than the screen filled with an enigmatic section of pavement. "Because there were guards everywhere, we had to be careful shooting and had to keep moving on," explained Wu, a suggestion of defensiveness entering his voice.

More agricultural fields with distant figures bent over in work followed. Then came another nondescript brick building and some more out-of-focus trees.

A new cassette. Another field. One more section of wall. A banal stretch of road.

I glanced over at Gelber. He had started tugging at his hair, a nervous tic he had when he grew anxious.

"OK! This is it!" exclaimed Wu, sensing the deflating mood in the room. "Here come the prisoners!"

As several long lines of men with shaved heads digging a canal along a roadside flashed onto the screen, everyone sparked to life. Gelber even got out of his chair for a closer look at the monitor. But before the distant prisoners came fully into focus, they too dissolved into a blur.

Another cassette. More brick buildings behind brick walls, more gate signs in Chinese, and more nondescript fields sailed by. By then, everyone was watching with a silent sense of gathering fatalism.

"OK, now, don't miss this!" Wu exclaimed, as the last of his cassettes clicked into the video player. "Here's the tape Ching-li shot inside the Shanghai Laodong Steel Pipe Factory."

This time the screen showed nothing but blackness as muffled voices conversed in Chinese.

"In a minute!" Wu blurted out. "Just a little further!"

We heard the sound of Velcro ripping as Ching-Li evidently drew the patch back from the peephole in the shoulder bag that held their hidden video camera. A shot of a rather bare office blinked onto the screen.

"That's it!" interjected Wu. "That's the office where I negotiated the contract with prison factory managers to ship wrenches to the U.S.!"

Unfortunately, the upper half of the frame remained obscured by the Velcro patch on the camera bag, so that all we could see on the screen was the lower half of several prison officials' uniformed bodies. We all strained forward, as if trying to peer into a room through a half-opened window.

"Move up! Please move up!" I murmured, begging the camera to pan up. Instead, the Velcro patch flopped back down over the hole from which the lens peeked, making even the tantalizingly half images vanish into blackness.

Although the footage was frustratingly incomplete and poorly shot, the discussions that Wu had managed to record with prison officials selling tools were fascinating. He even got the manager and assistant manager of one of the factories to explain how they illegally exported prison-made tools into the United States.

"Do you export your products abroad?" Wu asked point-blank.

"Yes, we do," answered the assistant manager obligingly.

"Our annual export quantity is about 1.2 to 1.5 million pieces," added the manager proudly.

"And how do you get your tools into American markets without getting caught?"

"Well, our products are never exported directly," explained the manager. "We always go through an import-export company under the aegis of our Ministry of Foreign Economic Relations and Trade."

"But as far as I know the U.S. has laws against importing products made by prison labor," countered Wu.

"Yes, but you see we export indirectly!" the manager explained patiently.

"Then, I guess that's OK," Wu laughed caustically.

At the second prison, Wu and his wife actually succeeded in getting out onto the factory's workshop floor. But, this time their video camera mysteriously malfunctioned, and we were left staring at a totally blank screen as garbled voices spoke in Shanghai dialect over an industrial din.

From any journalistic perspective other than commercial television, Wu had scored an amazing reportorial coup: He had gotten into a PRC prison and convinced the prison's factory managers to admit that they were successfully and illegally exporting tools made with forced labor into the United States. However, *60 Minutes* was a commercial television network program, and Wu had failed to get what it needed most: well-composed and clearly shot visual imagery on video to accompany a damning audio track.

As the screening ended, Gelber and Hamilton stared blankly at the empty screen like two disappointed anglers dreaming of the enormous fish that had just shaken their lure. The bitter reality was that in all the hours of Wu's hard-won footage, there was not a single ten-second segment of commercially broadcastable video. Gelber's disappointment had turned to desperation.

"Shooting is our biggest mistake," acknowledged Wu with an evident sense of deep regret. He clearly recognized that he had missed the opportunity he had been hoping would redeem his whole life.

Before Wu left for China, we had gotten a CBS cameraman to help familiarize him with the two Sony Handycams he would be using. However, the man had evidently done little more than give Wu technical tips on how to focus, zoom in, charge and change batteries, and use the different buttons on the camera. Wu had not learned how to frame, compose, or hold a shot, all of which would have been almost impossible to do anyway with his camera hidden inside a shoulder bag that prevented him from being able to look through the viewfinder. Compounding the problem, we had allowed no time for him to practice shooting with a lens poking thru a peephole in his bag. And so, what was to have been Wu's crowning moment of triumph had turned into one of failure and humiliation.

As the senior producer who had sold the Chinese prison labor story idea to Don Hewitt at *60 Minutes*, Gelber was particularly unnerved. He was the one who would be held responsible for the hundreds of thousands of dollars that had been spent for naught. On the strength of Wu's anecdotal descriptions of his trip, we had all dared believe that the elusive footage needed for a convincing television segment was now miraculously in hand. But it was not. And now not only Wu's but everyone's else's dreams had been dashed. For a few more moments, we all just sat silently around the screen mourning the fact that Wu's hidden camera had proven so infuriatingly blind.

"What you did was brave and truly incredible," Gelber wearily, but magnanimously, told Wu. "We, of course, need facts, figures, and the evidence that you actually made it back to those camps to give our story journalistic integrity. But television is a visual medium where it's not enough for us just to get someplace and catch a glimpse or two that proves we were there. Finally, the camera must capture enough memorable scenes in a prolonged way to tell a visual story. The camera must be allowed to linger long after you've captured the simple fact that you're there, because what stays with a viewer is not the facts, but the visual memory of a place."

"But David, you don't know how dangerous it was!" interjected Wu plaintively. "It wasn't like shooting home video!"

"I understand!" replied Gelber patiently. "And as producer, I feel terribly remiss, because I should have known we couldn't send you out into the field on a dangerous mission like this with a hidden camera, but without real training in shooting and expect you to somehow come back with usable footage."

Wu nodded at this gracious mea culpa, but I could see he still blamed himself.

I too felt responsibility for this debacle. I had been so preoccupied with just getting the project together, getting us all into China and to the camps, that it had never occurred to me we might actually succeed in overcoming all these formidable logistical challenges, only to founder on something as basic as camerawork. Knowing nothing about shooting, editing, or TV programming, Wu's goal had been simply to get into his old camps, shoot a few establishing shots to prove he had actually been there, and then get out. He would tell the rest of the story himself.

Even though Wu was deeply apologetic and visibly discouraged, I could see that he was taking in all our reactions to what he had shot and the explanations of the kinds of images television producers needed to make a program convincing to American viewers. Alas, these lessons came too late and were now useless.

■ ■ ■

Because Hewitt could be volcanic when presented with bad news, Gelber dreaded the moment he would have to tell him what had happened to our much ballyhooed project. Although he had all but decided to fold the tent, Gelber still wanted to have one final ceremonial meal together as a farewell before he and Hamilton returned to New York and the unpleasant business of confronting their boss. So, Baifang and I suggested that everyone come out to dinner on our ranch in West Marin County. We imagined it as a kind of last supper.

Chapter Twelve

DEATH AND TRANSFIGURATION

AS BAIFANG AND I prepared this farewell meal, I was possessed by a sad sense of opportunity lost. The question of the Chinese Communist Party's historical mistreatment of its people had been an underreported story and it was heartbreaking that our months of effort had produced nothing. For now, political imprisonment and forced labor in China would remain terra incognita for most Americans.

In the United States, most Americans knew that slavery had once existed and simply viewed it as the way things were. Such was also the case in regard to "reform-through-labor camps" and prison labor in China: Most Chinese understood that political imprisonment had long been a reality and that it continued. However, few knew its full dimensions, much less how to change it. Now, I had to admit, neither did I. Maybe it was just how things had been and always would be. Perhaps it was naive for us as outsiders to have ever imagined we could do anything to alter this stubborn status quo in such a distant land, even with the cooperation of a person as knowledgeable and committed as Wu Hongda and with the global media clout of *60 Minutes*.

As I set the table for dinner, I tried to console myself with the knowledge that I had at least learned a lot. However, it was impossible not to feel deflated by the bitter reality that this Herculean effort had failed so abysmally. Despite its vaunted "era of reform and opening up," in many ways China remained as closed to the outside world and unchangeable as before America's effort to engage it began. We had been outsiders then, and in truth, we were still outsiders, hardly the first foreigners to have blunted our swords on "trying to change China."

It was a beautiful summer evening as everyone began arriving. As we sat down at our dining room table looking out over the Pacific Ocean toward China, no one quite knew how to broach the question of our unsuccessful effort, leaving a triste sense of failure hanging over the room. We were halfway through our meal when a long awkward pause interrupted our banter. Then, as if he had decided that our unsuccessful efforts deserved some sort of formal benediction, Gelber said, "Well, it was a very good try. I'm so sorry we were not able to be more . . . " But, because he did not know quite how to finish his thought, he stopped, plunging the room back into silence.

Then Wu unexpectedly put down his fork.

"OK!" he announced peremptorily. "I've made up my mind."

"About what?" asked a vexed Gelber.

"I'll go back to China."

"You'll what?" Gelber exclaimed in astonishment.

"I've decided!" continued Wu, a steely look now in his eyes. "I want to go back again to Shanghai and meet the managers in those two prison factories where we screwed up the video, and I want to try again. They wanted to sell stuff so badly that if I returned, I know they'd see me. So, I've made up my mind. I'm going back!"

A stunned silence gripped the table.

"I don't understand why you'd ever do that," exclaimed a flabbergasted Gelber.

"For them," replied Wu without hesitating. "For all the prisoners like me who've been in those camps and are still there. I want to tell the whole world about them, and this is my best chance. We should look at the trip I just made as a practice run. Next time I'll be less nervous, more confident, better able to understand the current circumstances, and I'll know what I'm doing with the camera." He smiled.

"It would be incredibly dangerous!" exclaimed Gelber, "but we could give you some real lessons in shooting, and . . . "

"Why not?" responded Wu with some of his former elan.

"If you returned," pressed Gelber, "do you think we could arrange for Ed Bradley and a CBS crew to meet up with you somewhere in China and shoot a few scenes together?" Now Gelber too seemed gripped by a renewed hopefulness.

"No problem," Wu shot back. "If you can get Bradley a visa!"

"Do you think there'd be any way for Bradley to get into the Qinghe or Tuanhe camps to shoot a few moments with you reminiscing about being imprisoned there?" The questions had begun to tumble out of Gelber, each more extravagant than the last.

"Anything is possible," replied Wu.

"OK," continued Gelber, looking Wu right in the eye. "Let me ask you something that may just be too ridiculous. Do you think there would be any chance we could get Bradley into a meeting with some of those prison factory managers? You know, maybe have him pose as the head of a U.S. trading company wanting to order some goods in China?"

"Sure," replied Wu, sensing the CBS hounds were back on the scent.

"Goddamn it!" exclaimed Gelber. "This could be great!"

He and Wu had become so possessed by the idea of returning to China, it was difficult not to be swept up by their enthusiasm.

However, if Wu's willingness to expose himself once again to the system that had brought him so much suffering was heroic, it was also obsessive and frightening. Even when given a dignified chance to let go of this nightmare, he was unable to do what most other human beings would have done in a heartbeat. He could not just let the past be the past and walk away into a better future.

By then, my head, too, was spinning. Just as things seemed to have reached an end point, Wu had suddenly reinvigorated this whole madcap venture by agreeing to return to the dragon's lair.

"What can you possibly tell Hewitt?" I asked Gelber.

"Well," he began haltingly. "I suppose I could try to pitch another round as a kind of Act II." Then he turned back to Wu.

"Is what you're proposing really possible?" he asked.

"Anything's possible," Wu responded oracularly.

Frankly, I did not know what to think. If the whole idea had been farfetched in the beginning, it was even more so now. Moreover, with our baby coming soon, how could I re-up for another round? I certainly would not have considered doing so had I sensed any hint of opportunism or ambivalence in Wu's renewed commitment. Yes, he wanted to get even with his tormentors. Yes, he wanted to right past wrongs. Yes, he was seeking revenge. And yes, he was a man possessed. But these were all understandable human consequences of what had happened to him. That said, Wu had also come to impress me as someone who had learned how, despite all the challenges, setbacks, and failures, to keep holding onto hope by just soldiering on.

"Hope is like an intangible presence that can be neither affirmed nor denied," Lu Xun once wrote. "It's like a roadway. Originally there's not even a path. But, as many pass by, a path becomes a roadway" (希望本是无所谓有，无无所谓无的。这正如地上的路；其实地上本没有路，走的人多了，也便成了路).

■ ■ ■

As we waited for Hewitt's return from vacation to learn whether he had the stomach for yet another round in China and more expenditures, I found myself wondering what drove a person like Wu? Whence came his audacious tenacity to keep going and bearing witness?

The notion of "bearing witness" is deeply rooted in Judeo/Christian/Freudian culture, and it became more deeply explored and amplified as a result of the Nazi Holocaust in Europe. However, the idea of bearing witness was not one that had ever found widespread resonance among Chinese during either traditional or modern times. This recognition made me curious about the origins of Wu's own strong impulse to expose the Party's crimes against him and its people. I could not help wondering if his obvious impulse did not have something to do with the time he spent as a child in Shanghai schools run by the Jesuits. After all, he had told me that during some of his darkest times in the camps, he had often turned to his Catholic faith and God for succor.

To get a better understanding of the impulse to bear witness, I started rereading some of the works of Primo Levi, an Italian Jew who was interned in concentration camps by the Nazis during World War II but survived. After finally being freed from Auschwitz in 1945, he set about writing a series of haunting but insightful books about how human beings who bear the memory of savage persecution, suffering, and survival are damaged, but also sometimes strangely fortified. In many ways Levi's book, *The Drowned and the Saved*, seemed almost written for Wu. In it, he explored how shame and guilt often follow what he called "reacquired freedom," when a victim is finally released from his or her torment, but never from the character-shaping experience of it. In a most personal way, Levi analyzed the self-accusation mechanisms that haunted him after his release and the regrets he brought back with him from the camps because of all the fellow prisoners he felt he had "failed in terms of human solidarity," by "omitting to offer help" during their times of abject need. For Levi, the most agonizing question for a prisoner after release was "Are you ashamed because you are alive in place of another?"

Because Levi knew through firsthand experience that it was almost impossible for a survivor to erase the "suspicion that each man is his brother's Cain," someone who has "usurped his neighbor's place and lives on in his stead," he was never able to overcome his own deep sense of guilt for having "not done anything, or enough, against the system." Levi wrote about how, long after his release, guilt burrowed into his soul "like a woodworm," causing him unending suffering

By surviving China's labor camps, Wu too was elected into what Levi called the "saved" rather than the "drowned," or those who had lost their lives. But, Levi warned, such salvation left the saved forever confronting the question "Why me?" Racked with guilt for surviving, many felt compelled to do something in their later lives to justify having been saved.

Some similar psychological drama must certainly have been churning away inside Wu. Having figuratively escaped China's punitive embrace twice, his inchoate but powerful longing for atonement seemed to keep drawing him back again and again into the darkness in a relentless search for some way to deal with the unending guilt over having survived. As Levi solemnly observed, no matter how much penance is paid to the drowned, it is never enough to relieve the burden of guilt shared by those lucky few who were "enrolled among the saved." Being saved, wrote Levi, set him off on a "permanent search of a justification, in my own eyes and those of others."

Alas, search as Levi did for some way to justify his survival, he failed. He found himself caught up in a contradiction so unresolvable that death could be his only escape. In his case, when death finally came, it was sadly by his own hand.

But if suicide was Levi's only way out, I doubted it would be Wu's. His urge to bear witness impressed me as far too strong to allow him to forgo it. And he could only bear witness by staying alive, by testifying, as he had in the U.S. Congress, through his research at the Hoover Institution, and by undertaking projects like ours. Only through such activities did he seem able to overcome his despair and reaffirm his right to go on being alive. Indeed, before his first trip to China, he had often spoken with me almost scornfully about those in the *laogai* camps with him who, instead of fighting, committed suicide as an escape.

"Some people in the camps thought of suicide as a release from their suffering. I just thought to myself, 'Well, if I die, who will tell the truth about these camps?' " Then he paused for a moment before adding, "You know, we Chinese have an expression suggesting that when death comes to those who were wronged, they are so filled with regret they cannot close their eyes (死不瞑目). So, I always told myself, 'No! I will not give up! When I die, I need to be able to close my eyes!' "

As Levi wrote, "My religious friend told me that I survived so that I could bear witness."

■ ■ ■

One afternoon Wu again surprised me.

"I have to tell you something," he began abruptly as soon as I answered his phone call. "Sometimes I don't feel very good about what we're doing."

"What do you mean?" I asked, confused by his uncharacteristic tentativeness.

"I mean, I want to expose everything I can about this gulag, but at the same time there's something about deceiving people I don't like," he responded. "And, I also know that if this *60 Minutes* program ever airs, it will be the little people working in the prisons who helped me or were just doing their jobs who'll get in trouble, not the big leaders who really deserve it."

It was reassuring to know that despite all his years of abuse, Wu had not turned into a retaliatory mirror image of his tormenters. But I had no immediate solution for his dilemma. I asked him, instead, if he thought people in the PRC had been so defoliated of conscience by all the political pressures, betrayals, and violations of trust in the name of revolution that many had completely lost their sense of loyalty and trust.

"No," he answered emphatically. "Do you know where loyalty and trust survived?"

"Where?"

"In the labor camps among us prisoners. I've never encountered such loyalty! And it is precisely because I have such trust in those people's loyalty that I now dare go back to China. I know I can trust them and find help among them."

■ ■ ■

Don Hewitt arrived back from his vacation, and Gelber finally told him that we had failed to get enough usable footage to make a program. As feared, he expressed exasperation and threatened to cancel the project. However, Gelber believed he managed to convince him to leave the door open by reminding him of two things. First, given the impact of the debate raging between Congress and the president over China's rights abuses on the question of regranting Beijing's MFN trade status, a program like ours on forced labor in China could be extremely topical. Second, because on his last trip Wu had gained so much valuable in-country experience and developed so many good contacts, we had a much better chance of getting exceptional footage on a second trip. Amazingly, after a few days mulling things over, Hewitt relented and gave a green light for a second act.

When I told Wu, he smiled and said he felt redeemed. Then he asked whether I was still on board. In truth, I was completely divided. But given all that had already happened and the way our team had somehow stayed together during even the most difficult times, it was difficult to think of just dropping out. However, there was the question of our unborn child.

When I discussed the question with Baifang, she urged me to do what I felt was right. But I could feel that her tolerance was filled with ambiguity. So I decided to neither commit nor drop out. I would continue for now, see what happened and how she was, and make a final decision later. She said she understood, leaving me marveling anew at how such an understanding and faithful person ever emerged from Mao's revolution.

Chapter Thirteen

BACK TO WORK

WU WENT IMMEDIATELY back to work at Stanford's Hoover Institution on Peace, War and Revolution, building his database, mapping as many new prisons, their affiliated factories, mailing addresses, and phone and fax numbers as he could identify. This research enabled him to contact prison officials directly in hopes of getting some to respond and give him tangible evidence that prison enterprises were willing to trade with American businessmen. So, he began faxing prison factory managers, saying he was an American importer who planned to visit China soon and would like to meet and discuss doing business in person. I was worried that his last visit might have blown his cover, but he was so excited by these latest leads that he just shrugged off such concerns.

■ ■ ■

"OK!" Wu announced with great gusto a few days later.

"What's up?" I asked.

"I've made some important new contacts."

"Where?"

"Qinghai Province," he announced proudly.

"Qinghai?" I exclaimed, surprised that he would want to go all the way out to this very remote and sparsely populated western region.

"Yeah," he replied. "I just got a response from a prison factory in Xining that tans yak and sheep hides, and they actually want me to visit their factory! So, I've decided pay them a call."

The news that Wu had expanded his quest all the way to western China filled me with the same mix of excitement and worry that had kept my nerves on edge ever since we began this unlikely project. Qinghai Province was a remote region in between Himalayan range and the Tibetan Plateau, the Taklimakan and Gobi Deserts, and the sandy wastelands of Xinjiang Province. Because Qinghai hosted one of the PRC's most extensive networks of prison camps, many called it "China's Siberia."

"If you get in trouble out there," I protested, "it will not be easy to drop out of sight and escape."

"I know. But then, anywhere I go in China will be dangerous," he countered stubbornly, suggesting he was not dissuadable.

Wu's mention of Qinghai evoked memories of a trip I had made there in 1981. As part of his "reform and opening" agenda, Deng Xiaoping began opening up many long-closed Tibetan ethnic areas to foreign mountaineering and trekking groups as a way of earning much-needed foreign currency. Since I had always been interested in China's historically fraught ethnically Tibetan region, I joined an expedition attempting to summit Qinghai's 20,610-foot-high Mt. Amne Machin (阿尼玛卿山), one of the few remaining peaks of consequences on the planet that was still unclimbed.

During our weeks in Qinghai, we drove for days on arrow-straight dirt roads that lanced across vast expanses of alpine grasslands and deserts sparsely inhabited only by pastoral Golok nomads. Never had I seen a more desolate but also strangely beautiful landscape. The starkness of Qinghai's treeless mountains, barren grasslands, and endless desserts marked the province as a place of fathomless remoteness, emptiness, and isolation. It was precisely these qualities that made it a perfect place for prison camps. For even if an inmate somehow managed to escape the confines of a prison, it was all but impossible to escape the hostile surrounding wilderness. So, like Xinjiang, Qinghai became a favored place to send ideological criminals with long sentences. Soon prisons became one of the province's most important industries.

I vividly recall coming upon my first Qinghai prison camp. We had been driving across a vast flat stretch of grassland when the outlines of a fortress-like rampart rose on the horizon before us like a distant ship on a calm sea. Only as we drew nearer did I see that it was, in fact, a compound ringed by stamped-earth walls, fringed with barbed wire and turreted guard towers. As we passed, a long file of prisoners with shaved heads and wearing faded blue uniforms appeared trudging down the road. When I asked our Chinese Mountaineering

Association guide if they came from a nearby reform-through-labor camp, he just squeezed his eyes closed and shook his head, as if such a question was too forbidden to be addressed openly to a foreigner.

In 1991, Human Rights Watch (HRW) released a report, "Prison Labor in China," that should have ended all debate as to whether Chinese prisons factories and farms sought to sell goods and commodities produced with forced labor on global markets. HRW researchers had gained access to a restricted circulation journal published for Chinese prison officials that, in the most upbeat language imaginable, extolled China's prisons as playing a key role in a burgeoning export drive. Ding Banghua, an official in a provincial prison bureau, was even quoted as raising the question of whether reform-through-labor enterprises could and should develop "a foreign-oriented economy."

"The answer must be affirmative," Ding jauntily responded. "Some enterprises have already done so with flying colors," he continued. "After 30 years and more hardship getting started and vigorous development, *laogai* enterprises throughout the country have great potential for . . . earning foreign exchange." Then Ding candidly acknowledged that "nearly every province has its own sizable community of labor-reform enterprises."

Despite such brazen official self-admissions, Chinese officials still regularly insisted that goods made with forced labor were not being exported to the United States.

▪ ▪ ▪

Wu kept reminding me that several prison factories he had previously visited in Shanghai were eagerly awaiting his return. Indeed, he had even requested that one send samples of their tools inventory to him in California so he and "his boss" could check out their quality before visiting the factory.

"We got a good one!" Wu proudly proclaimed on our next call.

"One what?"

"Another response to my faxes."

"From where?"

"The Shanghai Laodong Machinery Plant, and it's even on letterhead signed by Factory Manager Lu Weimin and Vice Manager Lu Limei!"

They were the two unknowing stars of Wu's ill-fated first Shanghai video that showed only the bottom half of their bodies as they discussed a deal.

Wu faxed me the response he had just received from them. The first thing I noticed was that the opening lines of the letter were in English, albeit bowdlerized English, suggesting that the two managers were not unaccustomed to doing business abroad:

> To: Mr. Harry Wu.
> Re: Letter intented about socket, wrench, spanner, etc.

The rest of the letter was handwritten in Chinese:

"Our factory can manufacture hand tools in accordance with whatever trade-marks your company provides," it read. And to make the source of products even less traceable, they assured Wu, "it is also unnecessary for us to imprint our products with a *Made in China* stamp."

Wu sent back an immediate reply asking for "best prices" on seven different kinds of wrenches. He also asked if they were in a position to become "long term suppliers" to an American customer. Finally, he asked whether they would be available to sign a contract if he came to Shanghai in mid-August.

A response came right back: They were not only willing to become a long-term supplier but would welcome Wu to Shanghai for negotiations and a contract signing in August.

"Please let us know in advance of your arrival so that we can arrange a meeting more easily," they wrote.

They mentioned the name of the state-run export-import company in Beijing through which their prison-made goods were laundered for export. They also cheerfully added that they had already shipped tool samples to Wu in San Francisco, providing us with our first concrete evidence that goods were actually coming into the United States from Chinese prisons. Finally, these managers declared their eagerness "to discuss specific details face to face" in Shanghai.

If they were willing to meet with Wu, might they not also be willing to meet with his putative boss, perhaps even Ed Bradley posing as company president? Suddenly, I dared imagine Gelber's dream actually coming true: Chinese officials with a CBS *60 Minutes* anchorman masquerading as a businessman clinching a deal for prison-made goods destined for the United States . . . all on camera!

■ ■ ■

Filled with new energy and ambition, Wu planned to leave in two weeks for Hong Kong to prepare the way for Bradley, Gelber, myself, and a *60 Minutes* crew to follow. However, his grand plan depended on three uncertainties: First, he needed to get another visa for China, in Hong Kong where it was often easier to get approval than at PRC consulates in the United States. Second, I also needed to get a visa. And third, the *60 Minutes* crew would need an invitation letter from the Chinese government to get visas issued by the Chinese consulate in New York City.

Gelber's plan was to request a formal invitation from the Chinese government for a CBS crew to travel to Beijing and shoot a series of formal, sit-down interviews with ranking Chinese diplomats and trade officials. This would give them a chance to explain why they believed China deserved to have the U.S. Congress renew its unconditional MFN trade status. While the crew was in the country, Gelber also hoped to find a way to quietly break loose from official oversight to shoot with Wu in other locations as well. But hopes were only hopes. Gaining media access to China, especially for an investigative news program like *60 Minutes*, had always been a heavy political lift. Their investigative agenda made them immediately suspect.

If Wu succeeded in actually getting a visa in Hong Kong and then got into China, he promised to call me in California upon arriving at each new city. That way we would know he was safe. He had now received more camera training and had also devised a new, more detailed system of codes so that if we all succeeded in getting into China, we would be able to communicate more securely and effectively than last time. Wu would still be Peter, and I would be Jonathan. However, this time he wanted us to communicate via numbers corresponding to predetermined messages. As always, I was impressed by his tenacity, ingenuity, energy, and boldness. Of course, anyone who endured nineteen years in Chinese labor camps had been forged on an anvil of brutal Darwinian natural selection, a struggle that only the fittest survived.

▪ ▪ ▪

Wu was extremely agitated when he next rang.

"Yesterday someone with a foreign accent called the office of the company where I used to work here in California and asked for me by name," he reported. "When the receptionist said I was no longer employed by the firm, the caller refused to leave his name. I'm worried he was an agent for one of the prison factories checking up on me."

"But it could have been anyone," I countered.

"Yes, but remember I've been using my old company business cards only when visiting prisons in Shanghai," he responded. "And since I haven't worked at that firm for a long time, it would be very strange for anyone to call me at that number." After a pause, he added, "Or maybe one of the prison managers passed my name to the PRC consulate here in San Francisco, where officials certainly know me. If so, they may now realize that I've been in China and up to no good."

His concerns were reminders, if any were needed, of how fraught and dangerous another trip to China would be.

■ ■ ■

I had begun to notice that when Wu became worried, he often seemed to numb his fears with new injections of hyper-planning and activity. But every so often, he was unable to hold at bay the terrifying reality of what he was attempting and would lose his composure.

"You know, sometimes I get really scared," he confided a few days later. "I have no way of knowing what the Chinese government might have learned about my last trip. If I'm now on their radar and then go back, I could be walking into a huge trap. If I already had a U.S. passport, I wouldn't worry so much. But I'm still a Chinese citizen on a temporary U.S. travel document. So, should they catch me, I don't think they'd hesitate to . . . " He didn't finish his thought.

Until this conversation, I had not fully appreciated how much we had all come to depend on Wu's confident, sometimes even cocky, manner to pull us through all our own moments of uncertainty. I was usually the cautious voice, while he pushed on with unflinching resolve. When he too evinced trepidation, it was hard to know how to reassure him or avoid the conclusion that we were, in fact, engaged in an absurdly risky undertaking.

■ ■ ■

It was a lovely July day when Wu drove all the way out to our ranch north of San Francisco. He had insisted on one last face-to-face meeting before he left for Hong Kong.

"There's something I want you to keep for me," he confided upon arriving. Opening the trunk of his car, he took out a cardboard box and very solemnly handed it to me. "This contains all the materials I gathered on my last trip."

Then he gave me a manila envelope on which he had written, in both English and Chinese, "Don't open unless I've not returned by September 1st."

As I took the box and envelope, I had the unsettling feeling of being entrusted with someone's mortal remains.

■ ■ ■

Only hours before Wu was scheduled to leave home for the airport and Hong Kong, he called yet again.

"I think my phone's been bugged!" he whispered.

"What makes you think that?" I asked.

"Because over the last few days I've been hearing strange buzzing sounds. Then, this morning when I tried several different telephone sets on the same line to see if something was wrong with one of them, the buzz continued. However, when I plugged my phone into my fax line, it was clear."

"It might just be a bad line," I offered, wanting to do whatever I could to allay his anxieties at this penultimate moment.

"But if there actually is a tap, then they'd know all our plans . . . everything, and . . . "

I didn't want to feed his panic, but neither did I want to cavalierly dismiss the alarming possibility that the Chinese government did, in fact, have him under surveillance. It was no secret that it maintained elaborate networks of informants in the United States among Chinese academics and businessmen who kept close track of dissident political activities for the CCP. In fact, the Party's "United Front Department" (统战部) had been active abroad ever since the CCP was founded in 1921. Now, however, they were far better funded and organized than before. Even though U.S. relations with China had been quite friendly until 1989, Beijing's overseas surveillance and spy networks had become more robust, far more extensive than anything the Soviets had ever been able to deploy in the United States during their heyday. The PRC was now reported to have some 3,400 registered diplomats and commercial representatives, more than 75,000 students, and numerous other quasi-official emissaries in the country. And each was expected to give the Chinese government information if and when called upon to do so.

In fact, the FBI had become so concerned about this system of informants that in the winter of 1992 they began running ads in Chinese-language newspapers published in the United States appealing to immigrants to "help your new country" by reporting "any attempts or occurrence of harassment, intimidation or intelligence gathering" carried out by PRC operatives inside the United States.

"So, what do you want to do?" I asked Wu.

"Wait by your phone," he said and hung up.

Fifteen minutes later my phone rang again.

"I'm now at an outside pay phone," Wu said in a hushed voice. "After we hang up, I'll go right back home, and I want you to call me there. But when I answer, don't say much, just listen and agree with whatever I say."

When I rang Wu back, he immediately launched into a convoluted monologue about how glad he was that the U.S. Senate probably could not rally enough votes to override President Bush's expected approval of an extension of MFN trade status for China. He would be glad, he declared, to see China treated right and even be given permanent MFN status.

I understood what he was up to: He was laying down a trail of disinformation for whatever real or imagined eavesdroppers might be listening in. So, as he rambled on, I did nothing more than grunt occasionally in agreement.

"Good-bye," he said abruptly before hanging up.

Whether Wu was being sensibly cautious or excessively paranoid, I did not know. But the fact that he would soon be on a plane for Hong Kong, and then hopefully on his way into China, cast his cautiousness in a different light.

Chapter Fourteen

"PETER" GOES MISSING

AFTER WU HAD BEEN GONE for two days and I had still heard nothing from him, I grew worried. So, when Gelber arrived in San Francisco to go over our plans before my own departure, we decided we would try to call him at his Hong Kong hotel. We wanted to know if he had arrived alright, gotten a China visa, and had any further thoughts about the possibility of arranging a rendezvous for Bradley with Shanghai prison factory managers. If Wu had gotten a visa, he was not scheduled to leave for China until the next day. So, when we reached the front desk of his hotel and were told he had already checked out, we were alarmed. Then, just as we were anxiously discussing what do, the phone rang. It was Wu.

"I did succeed in getting a visa," he told us almost boastfully. "I got it through a China Travel Service tourist visa mill."

"Why did you check out of your hotel?" I asked.

"I switched hotels on the spur of the moment just in case I was being followed," he responded.

"And are you being followed?" I asked with no small alarm.

"I don't think so."

"And how are your spirits?" asked Gelber.

"OK," he said, but in a less than convincing tone of voice.

"When do you go in?" I asked.

"I have a ticket to Canton on the jet-foil tomorrow morning. And just in case something happens to me, I've sent photocopies of both my ticket and visa to you."

"But is everything alright so far?" I pressed.

"It's OK," he said in a subdued voice. "I'm just taking this one step at a time."

"You'll call as soon as you cross the border into China?

"Yes."

■ ■ ■

Knowing that Wu was scheduled to arrive in Canton by 10:00 p.m. Pacific Time, I waited in my office for his call. When midnight passed and the phone still had not rung, I began worrying.

1:00 a.m., no call.

2:00 a.m., still no call.

There are few things that make one feel more helpless than waiting beside a silent phone you hope will ring. I was just uncontrollably drifting off to sleep when I was awakened.

"Hello, this is Peter." It was Wu speaking without any inflection in his voice.

"Hi, Peter," I answered, relieved to hear his voice.

"For my wife's present, I think she'd prefer a size #1 dress," he began without any felicitations. "I could also take a size #12 for her friend." Then he hung up. My heart sank.

According to my numbered list of codes, "size #1" meant "I have arrived and everything is fine." However, #12 meant "There's something wrong that I have to work out. Wait for my next call."

While Wu was still in California, we had become accustomed to speaking openly, either in person or on the phone, almost every day. But now we were suddenly reduced to speaking in code, and only sporadically, on long-distance calls. After he hung up, I lay awake for several hours wondering what kind of trouble he might have run into in Canton.

Was he being followed?

Had he been right to suspect the Chinese government was bugging his phone?

Were Chinese authorities just waiting to arrest him at some incriminating place?

Such thoughts sent chills down my spine.

■ ■ ■

Soon enough, more unwelcome news came.

Doug Hamilton called from New York to report that the Ministry of Radio, Television and Film had turned down CBS's request for crew visas to shoot interviews with central government officials in Beijing. However, his contact at the Chinese consulate in New York told him that this was not necessarily a final refusal. In fact, he counterintuitively suggested that the crew consider going to China on tourist visas. To me, this seemed like very odd advice from a diplomat. Alternatively, the consular official said, CBS could communicate directly with the Ministry of Foreign Affairs in Beijing, present them with a detailed schedule and a list of officials whom CBS would like to interview, and request its sponsorship.

I immediately faxed a list of potential interview subjects to the ministry under CBS's name. Since we obviously could not mention our interest in prisons and goods made with forced labor, I simply indicated that CBS would like to send a crew and an anchor to Beijing "to explore various key issues relating to the MFN debate in Washington, D.C."

▪ ▪ ▪

According to his schedule, Wu should have arrived in Taiyuan, the capital of Shanxi Province, China's coal mine heartland, and should have called in. However, morning came and went without any word from him. Had something happened? All I knew was that he was scheduled to visit several coal mine camps where he had once been incarcerated.

That afternoon, copies of Wu's China visa and his boat ticket to Canton arrived via DHL. But, because he still had not called in, their arrival felt like something received from a soldier at the front who had gone missing in action since posting them.

I forced myself to stay awake in anticipation of his call. But as the night dragged and the phone did not ring, I grew increasingly uneasy. His suspicion that he had been under surveillance in California no longer seemed paranoid, only ominous. Unable to find out what was happening, I began wondering if we would ever hear from him again. Wu Hongda was still a Chinese citizen, so if officials were to arrest him, they would have no obligation to say anything to anyone. And if we ultimately did suspect he had been detained, what would we do? Such thoughts filled me with a dark sense of foreboding. Finally, I was so exhausted I fell asleep on the couch in my study.

■ ■ ■

As daylight broke, I jolted awake. Wu still had not phoned.

Evening fell again. Still no call.

It was now hard to banish my worst fears. Had "they" uncovered what he was up to and arrested him? Or had he been run down by a truck on a lonely road somewhere in coal country? Such "accidents" did happen and the Chinese government had no obligation to say anything to anyone about them.

The fact that the prevailing political climate in China remained deeply suspicious of foreign intentions was hardly reassuring. An article in Canton's *Nanfang Ribao* (南方日报), once a relatively liberal paper, did little to help my state of mind. It quoted propaganda officials as railing against foreign "reactionary forces" that they claimed had "stepped up their efforts" to "preach so-called democracy, freedom and human rights; to spread bourgeois values; and to incite hostile feelings against the Communist Party and socialism."

Indeed, this article seemed almost to have been written with Harry Wu and our *60 Minutes* project in mind. The Party did indeed believe that alien "counterrevolutionary elements" were tirelessly at work trying to subvert China's socialist state through what it called "peaceful evolution" (和平演变), quietly trying to precipitate "regime change" in a piecemeal, covert manner. And here they were not entirely deluded.

I tried to remind myself that it was dangerous to read such articles now and to focus on such dark thoughts, especially when exhausted and frightened. After all, unrestrained fears do have a way of blossoming uncontrollably into lurid waking nightmares.

■ ■ ■

As another night fell without a call, I somehow nodded off into a stuporous slumber. At 3:00 a.m., I was roused by the ringing phone. Snatching up the receiver, I was relieved to hear the kind of electronic beeps that signal an overseas call.

"Hello, this is Peter," announced a voice with complete serenity. "I think my wife would like a #5 size dress." This was our code for having returned safely from the coal mines in Shanxi to Beijing, and it flooded me with relief! At the same time, I was so upset that Wu had waited this long to call, I could not help sounding like a scolding parent.

"For heaven's sake, why didn't you . . . ," I started, forgetting all our codes. However, I quickly realized that such undisciplined directness was the road to perdition. Wu mumbled a few more codes, but I was so upset, tired, and also relieved to hear his voice that I just thanked him for calling, said good night, and hung up. And, for the first time in several days, I slept soundly.

■ ■ ■

The next morning, just as the sun was rising, the phone rang again.

"The Chinese Consulate finally agreed to accept our visa applications!" a voice barked. It was Gelber from New York.

"Wow!" was all I could muster.

"It's really coming together!" he said cheerfully. "FedEx your passport immediately, so we can submit all our visa applications together." I was greatly relieved to hear this news.

"And then what?" I asked.

"And then we want you to leave for Hong Kong this weekend. I'll follow with our cameraman, Norman Lloyd, on Monday or so. Then we can all strategize in Hong Kong for a few days before flying to Shanghai to reconnoiter with Wu. Finally, if we can get everything set up in Shanghai, we'll fly Bradley in from Tokyo."

"OK," I responded, not entirely convinced that things would continue to go forward quite as smoothly as Gelber seemed to be imagining. But he was in such a good mood, I was loath to inject any note of ambiguity.

"We've got to get Bradley on camera with those Shanghai prison officials," he continued. "That's the money shot! We gotta get it!" He laughed at his own crudeness. "And then I want soundman Ned Hall to go directly to Beijing with the equipment we'll need for the sit-down interviews with central government trade officials," he continued. "But before Beijing, I'd like Bradley to try to go unannounced with Wu and me to Tianjin and shoot some footage of Wu inside that Qinghe Farm camp where he was first imprisoned."

There was cinematic logic to Gelber's plans, especially trying to complete the sensitive shoot in the Qinghe camp before the full crew arrived in Beijing and the project became burdened with official government handlers from the Ministry of Radio, Film, and Television. Still, Gelber's insouciance about getting over all the hurdles that I still saw as possibly in the way worried me. To think that an American network TV crew could just march into a Chinese reform-through-labor camp, even one as enormous and dispersed as Qinghe, was naive! What Gelber had planned might work in Canada, but in the People's Republic of China?

■ ■ ■

When Gelber called again, early in the morning a few days later, he sounded strangely subdued.

"We picked up everyone's visa today, but . . . "

"But, what?" I asked.

"Well . . . your visa application was rejected," he somberly told me. "And when I asked the consular official why, he told me, 'Schell should not expect to go back to China now or anytime in the near future.' "

My heart sank.

As a younger man with most of my career still ahead of me, I had worried constantly about having my visa applications turned down. After all, who could purport to be a "China specialist" if they were unable to go China? So, the ability of the Ministry of Foreign Affairs to deny access gave it immense power over writers, journalists, scholars, and NGO staffers whose professional lives depended on being able to visit the country. Those of us who were vulnerable because of what we had been writing lived in constant fear of transgressing one of the Party's many ever-changing "red lines."

Ever since my first visa application had been delayed several years before, I had lived in a state of constant anxiety over being barred. With such a sword of Damocles always hanging over one's head, it was difficult to pitch book proposals to publishers, loft article ideas to newspaper or magazine editors, organize cultural exchanges, or even plan family visits. Threatened or actual denials of access allowed the Party to limit not only what was said, written, and broadcast by its own media inside China, but what was produced outside by foreign writers as well. This Party-sponsored system of intimidation represented a masterwork of extraterritorial control that was capable of keeping people like me in a constant state of anxiety about speaking out too honestly or writing too critically about China, even abroad, lest we be shut out.

Nonetheless, since the beginning of my association with China, I had always tried not to let fears of being punitively denied access influence what I did, said, or wrote. But it had been impossible to ignore the stark reality that the Chinese government could declare me—or any other China writer, journalist, scholar, NGO staffer, or businessperson—as "unfriendly" (不友好的) and then blacklist, detain, interrogate, expel, imprison, or excommunicate that person so that they could no longer do their work or make a living.

It was also telling that the first groups of foreign filmmakers, scholars, and journalists to be shut out tended to be those who spoke Chinese the best. The Party loved to wax eloquent about the virtues of "building bridges" and "mutual understanding." However, it was exactly those with the deepest understanding and connections to China who were the first to be excommunicated. The bitter irony for many of us was, the more we understood the Chinese Communist Revolution and "Marxism, Leninism and Mao Zedong thought," the more critical we became. And since our job was to write and speak honestly and publicly about what we had learned and come to understand, we easily became what Party parlance referred to as "poisonous weeds" (毒草).

There was only one small cryptic virtue to becoming a victim of such punitive treatment: It gave a foreigner a taste of what the Party had been regularly dishing out to its own people, chastising tens of millions of Chinese as "poisonous weeds," "bad elements," "counterrevolutionaries," "rightists," "capitalist roaders," "revisionists," "bourgeois elements," "enemies of the people," "hostile foreign forces," and the like, over the previous decades.

Of course, those designated as deserving of ostracism at one moment might be "rehabilitated" (平反) the next. But there were no guarantees. It was a capricious and brutal nonsystem that kept everyone off-balance and afraid.

While Gelber's news about my visa was discouraging, it was not entirely unexpected.

This was hardly the first time I had been ostracized. Over many years of going in and out of China, this threat had become a regular and elemental part of my life. Since, over the decades, I had written so many books and articles and done not a few films that were often critical of China, I had almost always been on some sort of political probation. But the fact that the threat was constant did not make it any easier to get used to it.

And not to be forgotten was the fact that I was married to a Chinese woman. This meant that when an insurmountable political wall was thrown up between me and China, the otherwise happy commons that had allowed us both to go back and forth between her homeland and my own was disrupted.

■ ■ ■

"I don't think we can pull this off without you," Gelber said dolefully when we spoke next. "For God's sake, I've never even been to China! I don't see how we can navigate all the difficulties that are bound to confront us alone."

"You should just plunge ahead," I replied numbly, not wanting to share the fullness of my own distress. "Wu's there waiting, and he knows what to do. Anyway, you can't turn back now."

"OK," he responded, but with little enthusiasm. "Still, I'd like you to come to Hong Kong with us and at least help us plan things from there."

"Let me think about it," I countered.

Despite his concerns, I actually did think that Gelber and the CBS crew would be able to navigate things on their own.

The crew had secured visas, approvals to do some official interviews had been secured, and Wu was already in-country. Moreover, should the crew get caught shooting video around a prison camp, they could much more easily plead ignorance without someone like me in tow. Of course, Wu could not feign any such innocence. If there was anyone who understood the rules of the road in the PRC, it was him.

However, I had one real concern. While I had come to trust Wu's reliability, competence, and commitment, I worried that my sudden absence from what had become a real collaboration might somehow throw him off. I knew how wary he and his generation could be, especially when it came to relying on people they did not know well and fully trust. Deception and treachery had conditioned them to distrust anyone they did not know to the core. Trust in the PRC has historically been in short supply. It was a deficit I repeatedly experienced with Chinese colleagues and friends, many of whom had learned through bitter experience that it was safer to remain cautious and distrustful, particularly with people they did not know well. And foreigners came with another huge liability: Because we were officially distrusted, ordinary Chinese knew to be extremely careful about their liaisons with us, lest retribution follow. What Chinese had long referred as "a crisis of trust" (信任危机) was one of the most deeply rooted consequences of the Chinese Communist Revolution. Despite his American exile, Wu Hongda was still a product of that revolution, especially when it came to the matter of trust.

▪ ▪ ▪

The consul's pronouncement, "Schell should not expect to go back to China now or anytime in the near future," rang in my ears for days. Such a blunt expression about a specific person was not said casually by Chinese officials. This dictum had an air of final judgment about it that left me feeling both violated and hopeless. I tried to remind myself that if the Party knew the full measure of what we were up to, they too would feel violated.

Nonetheless, such a rebuke left me thirsting for some sort of antidote against the sting of defeat and the feeling of helplessness that came with it. So, instead of just yielding, I decided to take up Gelber's offer and go to Hong Kong.

■ ■ ■

When Wu next called from China, he sounded full of new confidence. He proudly announced that he had just arrived in Xining, the capital of Qinghai Province, what he called "labor camp central." Because he said he was calling from the Xining Telephone and Telegraph Bureau, I became wary as he chattered on about his contacts in the prison factory that tanned yak and sheep hides. What had happened to his paranoia?

"Everything's fine, and I'll see you in Shanghai," he reassured me, so cheerfully that I did not want to tell him I had just been turned down for a visa.

"Let's just hope everything works out," I soberly demurred. But Wu was an intuitive wizard, able to pick up the slightest nuance in a changed tone of voice.

"Is everything still going according to schedule?" he asked somewhat hesitantly.

"Yeah. Everything's OK," I replied, trying to turn up the confidence level in my voice.

▪ ▪ ▪

While Wu had been roaming Qinghai, Ed Bradley had been vacationing at his Aspen, Colorado summer retreat. When he surprised me by calling, I immediately suspected Gelber had put him up to it. Having been on the margins of our project as it unfolded, Bradley was only dimly aware of what was going on. Since I didn't want to rattle him with too many nerve-racking details about my visa denial, our uncertain plans, and our video failures, I gave him only a brief overview of why the issue of Chinese prison labor remained relevant to the United States and what we hoped he might accomplish with the program as anchor . . . if we could get him to Shanghai.

"And how do all these Chinese prisoners relate to American viewers?" Bradley asked, raising the question that has always been present whenever American commercial television networks did any foreign news story.

"Well, we're investigating whether goods made by forced labor in China are being secretly exported into the United States and ending up in shopping malls to be unwittingly bought by American consumers," I responded. "No matter how cost competitive importing such products is, it is still a violation of U.S. law. And now there's a hot debate in Congress over whether to permanently extend MFN trade status to China and make these exports even more affordable and available to Americans. It's something President Bush would like to do, and the political debate over the issue should reach a crescendo in Washington just as this *60 Minutes* story airs."

As we chatted, I was struck by the fact that, even though he was the segment's putative "correspondent," Bradley knew very little about what we were doing. He had played almost no role in researching or developing the story. Our conversation reminded me how dissimilar print and television journalism are. Whereas an investigative print reporter would have been "on" a story like this from start to finish, a TV network anchor's role was quite different. Often he or she came into the production process only after much, or most, of the heavy research and reporting had already been done by producers like Gelber and Hamilton. Then an anchor like Ed Bradley got briefed and joined the process. Not infrequently, Bradley was simply handed a script of questions by his producer just before he met a key subject for an on-camera interview.

Finally, after all the video for the segment had been shot and edited, the anchor did a voice-over, albeit one that had been drafted by the producer, so that by airtime the program sounded as if the story was largely the reportorial product of the anchor.

While there were exceptions, of course, all too many TV newsmagazine anchors—referred to in the industry as "the talent"—served more like actors than journalists. Their job was to bring a story researched and reported by others to life for a television audience, much as a skilled actor might bring the character in a script for a play or film to life on stage or screen. The most important role for such TV anchors was to create a convincing simulacrum of a foreign correspondent at work in the field, when in actuality, only after a storyline had been largely developed and reported by producers did the job of this kind of "correspondent" begin. Bradley's charge was to bring himself to life on screen as a character with enough dramatic punch and authority to make viewers want to believe the investigative drama he was presenting.

That said, it is important to note that such acting is hardly less demanding than actual reporting; it just involves a different kind of talent and skill set, the ability to play, rather than be, an investigative TV reporter.

Unlike Ed Bradley, other *60 Minute* anchors—Morley Safer, Lesley Stahl, Dan Rather, and Mike Wallace—frequently did participate more actively in reporting their stories. But they also knew how to play their on-screen roles in a convincing way.

■ ■ ■

As I prepared to leave for Hong Kong, a column came out in the *People's Daily* that seemed to speak directly to the people of that remnant British colony. It proclaimed that "the capitalist system just cannot be compared with the superiority and moral excellence of socialism." It also decried how "some youth blindly worship the so-called 'freedom and democracy' of the West and chase after a Western bourgeois lifestyle," while "their thinking remains empty and their spirit decadent." The article was a reminder that even as Hong Kong and South China began to merge economically into one regional marketplace, a vast gulf still divided them into two clearly demarcated and conflicting political universes.

■ ■ ■

As my departure day neared, I sensed Baifang's growing uneasiness. The ups and downs of this project had left her increasingly apprehensive. And with a baby coming, it was hard for her to have me leave home. Since she was not due for more than a month and I did not anticipate being gone for more than ten days, I urged her not to worry. But, having grown up in China, she knew firsthand how draconian the CCP could be, especially when dealing with dissenters and intrusive foreigners who deigned to meddle in what Party leaders considered China's "internal affairs." Still, she stoically uttered no word of complaint.

Chapter Fifteen

PERSONA NON GRATA

ON THE WAY TO HONG KONG, I could not help reflecting on the status of this anomalous "Crown colony" that had been ceded in perpetuity to Great Britain by the Qing Dynasty after its humiliating defeat in the first Opium War of 1841. Since then, this enclave had clung to the South China coast like a barnacle on the hull of a huge ship. However, in six years it was slated to be returned to "the embrace of the Chinese Motherland" (回归祖国怀抱). In negotiations with UK Prime Minister Margaret Thatcher, Deng Xiaoping had promised that Hong Kong would be allowed to coexist alongside China as a "special administrative region" under a unique formula of "one country, two systems" (一国两制) that seemed to guarantee it "a high degree of autonomy" for fifty years.

Nonetheless, come 1997 the world would lose this cavity of free expression and British common law that for a century and a half had afforded Chinese political refugees a haven from

China and foreigners a toehold on the South China coast that was "Chinese," yet outside Beijing's powerful field of political gravity. As our plane flew over Hong Kong Harbor to land at Kowloon's Kaitak Airport, the city seemed so immutable that it was hard to take in the reality that things would soon change dramatically, although nobody quite knew how.

I found Gelber and the cameraman Norman Lloyd at the Mandarin Oriental Hotel ready for a group dinner. As we ordered, Lloyd showed us one of his "lipstick lenses," an optical device capable of shooting wide-angle shots through a slender, bullet-shaped lens that he had rigged to peek out of holes in briefcases so that we could secretly film interviews with Chinese prison officials . . . if Wu could arrange them.

Toward the end of our dinner, Gelber leaned forward.

"You know, Orv," he began, "I'm still worried about navigating China alone. Is there any way for you to get a visa here in Hong Kong?"

"Well . . . ," I began, not wanting to encourage him, "I am very dubious I would succeed here in Hong Kong, but I could go to Macau and try there. However, I'm not optimistic."

Macau was Europe's oldest colony in East Asia. It had been leased to Portugal in 1557, lay sixty kilometers across the Pearl River Delta, and was known to be somewhat more lax in border controls than other crossings.

"You should try," Gelber urged. "Go first thing tomorrow morning and see what happens."

■ ■ ■

At 6:00 a.m. I was at the ferry dock ready to board a catamaran for Macau.

As we neared the Outer Harbor Ferry Terminal, an announcement came over the PA in Portuguese. There were a doubtless a few people from the old country still living in this historically anomalous territory where Lisbon and Beijing continued to act out their old roles. However, what they now shared was not so much an interest in trade as an interest in gambling. Casinos in Macau had proliferated and were pulling in an immense amount of wealth both for this retro colony and the PRC. But largely because of all this new gaming, Macau had lost most of the romantic old-world charm and grace it once had as Europe's earliest outpost in China.

Even in the 1960s, the colony's lovely tree-lined *avenidas* and balconied *pousadas* looking out over the old harbor had not been completely despoiled. Then, when the Zhuhai Special Economic Zone (SEZ) was established by Beijing just across the border during the go-go 1980s, new high-rise towers and garish casinos festooned with blinking neon began appearing. marking Macau's final transformation from old-world colonial relic to yet another new-world commercial wasteland supercharging the PRC with economic energy.

From the ferry dock, I walked to the China Travel Service office. There, a clerk told me that if I wanted to secure a visa in time to return to Hong Kong that night, I should go directly to the border, pass through Portuguese customs, and apply directly at the Chinese immigration office on the frontier.

Not quite sure what I was in for, I took a taxi to the border. After passing through Portuguese emigrations without incident, I suddenly found myself staring up at a crimson Chinese flag emblazoned with five gold stars flying in front of a cement and tile building that sat astride the two-lane highway connecting Portuguese Macau and Chinese Zhuhai. As I entered, my heart began racing. What happened here would determine whether I made it back into China. Then it occurred to me that paradoxically I was already in China, albeit provisionally and without a visa.

It did not calm my nerves to recollect that the last time I had been at this very border crossing, in the winter of 1981, I was here with my friend Tiziano Terzani, the well-known Italian journalist who was then based in Beijing for the German newsweekly *Der Spiegel.* Terzani and I had been traveling together around Guangdong Province trying to make sense of all the rapid economic changes that Deng Xiaoping's reform movement was unleashing on Southern China. At dinner one night in Taishan, we suddenly realized that it was New Year's night. Spontaneously, we decided to leave China through Macao and head to Hong Kong, where Terzani's wife and two children were living. However, we did not realize that the Ministry of Public Security did not like what Terzani had been writing and had been following him ever since we left Beijing.

Innocently, I went through customs ahead of Terzani without any problem, then sat down in the waiting room on the Macau side with a book, waiting for him to follow. When after an hour he still had not emerged, I asked a Chinese customs official what had happened. He just waved me off.

It was not until 2:00 a.m. that a furious Terzani finally emerged. He told me that Chinese customs officials had detained him because of a small bronze Buddha he had been given years ago in Phnom Penh where he was covering the war in Indochina and had carried with him ever since as a good luck charm. They had accused him, he said, of illegally smuggling antiques out of China.

As it turned out, the troubles we encountered that night at the Macau border were only the beginning of a longer saga for Terzani. When several days later he returned from Hong Kong to Beijing, where he was a resident correspondent, he was detained again at Capital Airport. This time he had his passport confiscated and was held under house arrest in his apartment for the next few weeks before being expelled permanently from China.

Now, here I was back again at this same border flooded with these unsettling memories.

Following a sign that said "Foreign Visa," I went up a graceless cement staircase to a landing adorned with an aquarium whose only evidence of marine life was a dense plume of green algae. Inside an office behind the aquarium sat a single customs official.

"I'd like to apply for a visa," I told him as jauntily as I could. He handed me a form.

I filled it out and handed it back to him with my passport.

"Just waiting a moment," he replied in stilted English as he strode purposefully into a back room.

There was something so backward about this office that I momentarily dared hope that word of my political disfavor had not yet electronically arrived here from Beijing or New York. However, when the agent sat down at a computer, my heart sank.

Ten minutes later he called out, "Schell!"

"Yes," I replied, expectantly.

"We may not grant you a visa." He slapped my passport down on the counter with finality.

"Why not?" I asked.

"No reason," he replied.

As I descended the dingy stairway again, despite the fact that I was still in China, I felt as cut off from it as when I had first arrived in Hong Kong in 1961 and "Red China" was a completely forbidden territory for Americans. Indeed, our U.S. passports were then officially stamped: "Not Good for Travel in the People's Republic of China." Now, after having made an uncountable number of trips there during the open period of the 1980s, barriers had come back up, at least for me. I was persona non grata . . . once more?

■ ■ ■

In Hong Kong the next morning, when I had breakfast with Gelber and recounted my Macau saga, he became very downcast. Although he did not say so, I sensed that he too was now beginning to wonder whether this whole venture could ever succeed.

■ ■ ■

On my fourth day in Hong Kong, Robin Munro, the locally based British research associate for Human Rights Watch, and

I had coffee together. When he told me he had just returned from both Beijing and Inner Mongolia, I was surprised.

"How did you ever get a visa?" I asked. International human rights organizations were not beloved in China, particularly Human Rights Watch, as I had learned the hard way from my ill-fated talk for the Beijing Foreign Correspondents Club.

"I confess I was amazed to get it," admitted Munro. "I was equally amazed that once in China, I did not detect any signs that I was being followed or that the government knew I was there."

Of course, the ministries of Public Security and State Security cannot be everywhere all the time. However, when they do decide to select someone for scrutiny and/or punishment, they can be relentless. Yet despite Munro's very high profile work for Human Rights Watch, he had somehow escaped their scrutiny.

As I was telling Munro about our *60 Minutes* project, my own visa rejection in New York City, and my ill-fated trip to Macau, he interrupted me.

"You know," he began, "the tour group organizer who somehow got me my visa is . . . Well, I'm not sure how she did it, but she came through. Maybe you should call her?"

"It's possible they're onto me," I replied. "And I don't want to attract any more attention than necessary to our *60 Minutes* venture or Harry Wu. So, maybe it's just not wise to . . . "

"But let me at least call her for you!" insisted Munro almost playfully. "I mean, why not? If they give you a visa, go! It's perfectly cricket."

Having become resigned to my visaless state, the thought of reigniting hopes only to have them dashed once again was not enticing. Nonetheless, I consented to let Munro call his contact. There was a remote chance that I might still prevail in the colony's transactional visa mill where the Hong Kong China Travel Service was known for recruiting any foreign tourist it could get its hands on to join what had come to be known pejoratively as Sea Slug Tours, group trips to China on which members invariably got treated to a banquet featuring braised sea slugs.

An hour later, a Miss Tan arrived in the lobby of the Mandarin Oriental Hotel and in a businesslike fashion asked me to fill out an application form, give her a photo, pay a fee, and hand over my passport. When she departed, I stood in the middle of the lobby for a few moments wondering if I would ever see my passport again.

Then Gelber announced that, instead of just sitting here in Hong Kong, he wanted me to go to Japan.

"Bradley's just sitting in Tokyo waiting to leave for Shanghai, if we can arrange it," he explained. "I think it would be helpful for him to have a full briefing from you about what we've been doing, why we're doing it, and what the implications are for Washington. Someone needs to update him, let him know that Wu's already in Shanghai trying to set up a sting operation with those prison officials he met on his first trip who still want to sell him tools made in their factory. Who knows if Wu will succeed, but if he does, Bradley needs to know that he will be posing as a CEO from the United States who's come to Shanghai to negotiate a deal. Above all, he needs to know just how sensitive everything is."

Even though I was very ambivalent about rushing off to Japan at the last minute, I agreed to go. So, I had to run out to a nearby travel agent and pick up an airline ticket to Tokyo.

Once I got back, Gelber wanted to go over all our plans, flight schedules, hotel reservations, dates, codes, rendezvous points, pseudonyms, and interview questions, so I would have an updated list for my Bradley briefing. By the time we finished, I was so burned out, I retreated to my room for a quick nap before my late-night flight to Japan. However, just as I was drifting off to sleep, the phone rang.

"Hello!" I snapped, irritated at being disturbed.

"Mr. Schell?" a woman's accented voice asked.

"Yes?" I responded warily.

"I'm in the lobby."

"Excuse me, but who are you?" I challenged, unable to disguise my impatience.

"Miss Tan. I'm here with your passport."

"Oh . . . my passport!" I blurted out, suddenly realizing that in the rush to get ready to go to Tokyo, I had put this important detail completely out of my mind. Of course, without my passport, I would not have even gotten out of Hong Kong, much less to Japan! Then, I also suddenly recalled my China visa application. "And . . . what about the visa?" I asked tentatively.

"No problem," she replied. "Meet me in the lobby."

I hurried downstairs, and there was Ms. Tan with my passport, open to a spanking new China visa. Stunned, I thanked her profusely and then immediately called Gelber on the concierge's phone.

"Guess what?"

"What?"

"I got a visa!"

"Way to go!" he congratulated. "How the hell did you do it?"

My head was spinning. Not only did I now have to cancel the flight I had just booked to Japan, but I had to quickly figure out how to get to Shanghai.

When I was sitting in that first class in Chinese history back at Harvard as an undergraduate, had someone told me that one day I would find myself in Hong Kong trying to infiltrate the People's Republic of China as part of a covert investigation of the Chinese Communist Party's prison gulag, I would have thought them barking mad. But here I was!

Somewhat hesitantly, I called Baifang. I wanted her to know that I had gotten a visa, but also that I would be back in time for the birth. However, when our home phone picked up, all I got was her voice on our answering machine message. The thought that I might have to leave Hong Kong without speaking to her left me so rattled that if the Ministry of Foreign Affairs in Beijing had called just then to notify me they had discovered my visa application, made a gross mistake, and decided to revoke my visa, I would not have minded.

Chapter Sixteen

NOT A SEA SLUG TOUR

AT 4:00 A.M., the alarm went off. I leaped out of bed, feeling less than refreshed. When I opened the curtains, dawn was just tingeing the cloud-studded sky over Hong Kong Harbor with pink. The frenzy of jet-foils, police cutters, ferries, junks, freighters, cruise ships, and American war vessels that usually plied this narrow channel by day had not yet begun, and the harbor's calmness made it look almost frozen.

Hastily I packed my things, checked out of the hotel, boarded the Star Ferry, walked to the Kowloon train station, and bought a ticket to the border. The Kowloon-Canton Railway was the same train I had taken on my first trip to China almost two decades before, when Mao was still alive and the Cultural Revolution had not yet ended. My many subsequent trips had all been via air, but none had been so filled with anticipation as that first one in 1975. Although I would now be returning to a place I had come to know well in the intervening years, this trip was so infused with tension, I felt as if I was headed not to a familiar place, but into the molten core of a nuclear reactor.

As passengers disembarked from our train at the Shenzhen border and flooded toward Hong Kong passport control, my heart was pounding so hard I was sure others could hear it. Making matter worse, even though it was not yet 8:00 a.m., it was so hot and humid, sweat was pouring off me. I got through Hong Kong emigration without incident. However, by the time I lined up for PRC immigration, my shirt was so drenched, I felt as marked as Hester Prynne by her scarlet letter.

Suddenly, it was my turn at the immigration booth. The Chinese customs official took my passport, opened it with a deft flick of thumb and forefinger, stared at my photo, and then at me with unreadable eyes. I tried to smile, but managed no more than a wan grin. Just as I thought my heart might burst, he reached for his entry stamp, raised it, let it hover over my open passport for a terrifyingly indecisive moment, before bringing it down with a satisfying thunk, leaving a neat vermillion seal on my visa.

Next came a baggage X-ray station. A surly young policewoman motioned me to put my suitcase on a belt for inspection by a scanning machine that looked like Fat Man, the first atomic bomb. As it emerged at the other end of the belt, she gruffly ordered, "Open!" Upon seeing my laptop, she arched an eyebrow. "Turn on!" she demanded. My screen flickered to life. "Passport!" she ordered.

For several minutes she inspected it, then officiously walked away, making me fear she had discovered something amiss.

However, I was relieved not to spot any computer monitors nearby. Anxiously I waited as she presented my passport to her chief. For what seemed like an eternity, he studied it. Then, without changing facial expression, he remanded it back into her hands.

"OK," she said and handed back my passport.

The gate that had been so irrevocably shut only a day ago had now miraculously opened. However, I felt little relief, much less exhilaration. I still had to get to Shanghai.

Outside in the hot, fetid, tropical air, the hectic din of China's foremost Special Economic Zone was deafening. Shenzhen was one of the original four SEZs set up in 1980 as part of Deng's vaunted "reform and opening" (改革开放) under the tutelage of Xi Zhongxun, the just "rehabilitated" father of China's future leader, Xi Jinping. During a single decade, Shenzhen had been transformed from a lazy fishing and farming village into a boomtown of more than two million people. With its noise, clutter, prostitutes, construction, and preening modern high-rise buildings, Shenzhen was neither Hong Kong nor China but a strange hybrid portending what was to come for much of the rest of China.

Outside the train station, I trolled through a scrum of private vehicle and taxi drivers waiting for fares until I finally found one willing to take me on the four-hour trip to Canton for a reasonable fare. From there, I planned to fly to Shanghai.

As my "Luminescent Pearl" (夜明珠) taxi pounded along the potholed road, we passed through a free-fire zone of Leninist/capitalist private factories. Trash blew in the wind, chemical green and red effluent gushed from outfall pipes into the surrounding rice paddies, a thick coating of grit covered everything, and a beige penumbra of smog hid the sun.

By the beginning of the 1990s, some 70 percent of China's industrial growth was coming from the kinds of joint venture companies and privately owned small and medium-sized enterprises (SMEs) that lined industrial corridors like this one between Shenzhen and Canton. Never mind equity, labor rights, health-care benefits, paid vacations, employee housing, environmental regulations, job security, or other such niceties. What fueled this Sinic version of cowboy capitalism was profit, profit, profit. Child labor might have been rampant, the natural environment might have been getting despoiled, officials might have been grafting their way to riches, and prisons might have been profitably exporting goods abroad, but businesses were moving manufacturing and jobs from America to this pulsing heartland of "socialism with Chinese characteristics" because costs were low and there was money to be made! And most of this region's neo-socialist/capitalist Chinese entrepreneurs were in no mood to hear chatter about the injustice of prison labor, much less airy questions about human rights violations.

By the time I arrived at Canton's White Cloud Airport, I was spent. After booking an evening flight to Shanghai, I got a cubicle at a micro-hotel and crashed for a few hours before I took off.

When I finally landed in Shanghai, it was difficult to believe I had made it. I had purposely decided not stay at the luxurious Portman Shanghai Hotel with the rest of the CBS crew because I did not want to risk having the Public Security

Bureau find me registered in the same hotel with them. Instead, I checked into a small Sino-Japanese joint venture hotel whose lobby was overrun by a tour group of young women from Tokyo, all wearing the same chamber pot–shaped hats.

After quickly dropping my suitcase in a Lilliputian-sized room, I grabbed a cab to the Portman. It was then an elegant new forty-story joint venture colossus featuring water flowing down one exterior glass wall and a lobby boasting a giant nugget-shaped gold sculpture, an apt symbol of China's new fixation on wealth. The hotel's impressive decor, its managers in formal morning coats, and the soft classical music that wafted through its lobby made it hard to believe that one was still in a police state where a Public Security Bureau, reform-through-labor camps, and ever more sophisticated systems of surveillance were everywhere.

Gelber had flown directly from Hong Kong. When I found him in his room, he was relieved I had made it without incident. When he told me that Wu too had arrived and was upstairs, I went up to find him. Upon exiting the elevator, I was relieved to see that the attendant on his floor was temporarily absent. Surveillance by round-the-clock attendants on each floor of major hotels was an old Communist tradition in the PRC.

When I knocked on Wu's door, a fleeting shadow moved behind the peep hole. Then, the lock turned, the door opened, and for a moment Wu just stood and stared. Then a huge smile broke out on his face.

"Son of a bitch (他妈的!)!" he said in Chinese. "You actually got here!"

After a fraternal hug, he hustled me inside, locked the door, and turned on the TV to muffle our conversation, in case the room was being bugged. Then, we sat down to talk, albeit in whispers.

"What caused you to give me that warning from Canton?" I asked, unable to restrain myself. "Why didn't you call me for so many days? I mean, how . . . "

"When my boat from Hong Kong landed at the dock in Canton, two customs officials pulled me aside and started questioning me," he began, speaking so softly I could hardly understand him. "As soon as they saw my U.S. reentry permit, they wanted to know if I was still a Chinese citizen. When I admitted I was, they demanded to know why I wasn't using my Chinese passport to 'return to the motherland.' I explained that it had expired. So, they wanted to know why I hadn't renewed it. What could I say? Finally, they asked what I'd been doing when I'd lived in China, when I had left, why I'd gone to the U.S., what I had been doing there since, why I had now come back, and who I was going to visit on this trip. The extent of their questioning was alarming, because I couldn't tell if they knew nothing or knew everything and were just playing cat-and-mouse with me. So, I didn't dare lie. I had to risk telling them something close to the truth. I even told them I'd spent time in a reform-through-labor camp in Shanxi and was now going back there to visit the chief who was my friend. Then, as suddenly as they'd begun interrogating me, they let me through. But when I called you, I was still unsure whether or not someone might be following me."

"Did you get any good video footage inside the mines?" I asked, changing the subject.

"The mines were flooded by heavy rains, so I couldn't shoot inside," he sighed. "But I did get some on-camera interviews with ex-prisoners. Then, I went out to Lanzhou in Gansu Province to visit the Lanzhou No. 2 Reform-Through-Labor Detachment that makes bus chassis. I told them I was an American Chinese businessman working in the transit sector and was interested in buses. Since their managers were dreaming of breaking into the foreign export market, they were thrilled to talk with me. After that, I took a train to Xining in Qinghai!"

As Wu regaled me with all his exploits, I became aware of a rancid smell that was utterly out of place in this luxury hotel. Then I spotted its source. In one corner of Wu's room was the skull of a long-horned gazelle with some meat still on the bone, sitting on top of several animal hides.

"Oh yeah!" Wu exclaimed, following my gaze. "I got those at the Qinghai No. 2 Reform-Through-Labor Detachment, the Qinghai Hide and Garment Factory that tans sheep and yak hides. There I shot prisoners with shaved heads wading around in huge vats of toxic tanning chemicals, signed a contract with the manager for 200,000 square feet of lambskin, and they wanted me to invest half a million dollars in their factory!" Wu laughed and threw up his hands in amazement. Then, as if he were a leather merchant proffering a sample to an interested customer, he handed me a soft sheep fleece to feel.

After spending nineteen years in such camps himself, and then almost a decade researching and writing about them in the United States, Wu had finally managed to start turning the tables on his former oppressors, and the experience was clearly making him quite jubilant.

■ ■ ■

When Bradley arrived from Tokyo, we slipped upstairs to his suite one or two at a time so as not to attract undue attention. I went with Wu, who proudly told Bradley that he had been able to arrange for several ranking Shanghai prison officials to come to the Portman Hotel and meet with him as Wu's "American boss." He also told Bradley that the prison wanted to sign a contract for a substantial order of tools to be exported back to the United States.

A knock on the door made us stop our talking. But it was only Gelber, who wanted to update us all on plans for videoing the discussions and the contract signing. "The Shanghai Sting," as he had taken to calling this shoot, would have several cameras in briefcases fitted with lipstick lenses peeking through small holes unobtrusively positioned around a special hotel suite.

One might imagine that anyone's pulse would have quickened at the prospect of secretly videotaping Chinese prison officials in the last mega–Communist-bloc country selling illegal tools *in flagrante delicto* to a putative American CEO. However, Bradley seemed untouched by any sense of excitement, much less the kind of anxiety and fear that had been putting the rest of us into a state of high dudgeon. In fact, Bradley seemed so unaffected by the audaciousness of Wu's plan that I felt quite ridiculous suggesting we turn on the television set as we talked, lest an eavesdropping device picked up our conversation.

We explained to Bradley that our meeting with the officials from the Shanghai Laodong Steel Pipe Factory would take place tomorrow morning and that both he and Wu would be outfitted with hidden wireless mikes connected to our hidden cameras.

We also informed him that Wu would greet the prison officials in the hotel lobby before ushering them upstairs to the special suite where Lloyd would be waiting, posing as his assistant. Then, after plying them with snacks and going over the terms of a deal for a tool shipment to the United States, Wu would summon Bradley as his company's president who had come all the way to China to meet his new Chinese partners. In discussing the pending deal, he would acknowledge that he was aware of the "special nature" of the Shanghai tool plant as a prison operation, but express his willingness to do business anyway.

We urged Bradley to remember that he should, as off-handedly as possible, ask his new Chinese "partners" to explain how any transaction would be laundered through a state-run Chinese export-import company to mask the illegal origin of prison-made goods. Finally, we urged him to inform his Chinese "counterparts" that, while his company was willing to do business with them, his "assistants," Wu and Lloyd, would need to inspect the factory's production line to satisfy their concerns about "quality control." Finally, we explained that as soon as the negotiations were over, Bradley and the CBS crew would race to the airport to catch a 6:00 p.m. flight to Tianjin. There Wu had rented a van so they could try to drive Bradley, Gelber, and the crew onto the Qinghe Farm to get some establishing shots at this camp in which Wu was twice incarcerated. Finally, Bradley, Gelber, and the crew would go on to Beijing to meet their official Chinese government hosts and do the formal interviews already scheduled with central government trade leaders.

Bradley took this all in with remarkable calm, asking only a few cursory questions. He radiated the air of someone used to being taken care of and trusting his subalterns to make things work out. He was what people in the TV news industry called "producer reliant." While his equanimity was reassuring, his obliviousness to the sensitivity of our situation was not.

Indeed, the foremost thing on Bradley's mind seemed to be getting to the hotel's well-equipped gym to work out on a Stairmaster. But since he was in Shanghai unbeknownst to the Chinese government, Gelber and I both felt that it would be extremely risky for him to appear in any public spaces. After all, he was a well-known media figure, and if recognized by any of the numerous American guests staying at the hotel, the Chinese managers might become alerted to his presence. The fact that such a famous U.S. television personality was in the hotel would surely require them to alert the Public Security Bureau.

"I think it might be best just to lie low tonight," counseled Gelber, using his best producer-talking-to-anchorman bedside manner.

"You don't expect me to stay imprisoned in my room all night, do you?" Bradley indignantly challenged. "Nobody tells me when I can and can't use a Stairmaster!"

"Well, it's up to you," shrugged Gelber, obviously a veteran of such exchanges. "But we just can't afford to have you recognized by anyone." An African American who was six feet tall was hard to miss in Shanghai.

Despite Gelber's pleas, Bradley headed straight to the gym as soon as our meeting ended. And while he was there, several Americans did, in fact, recognize him. One even sent a fruit basket up to his room with a card saying, "Welcome to China."

■ ■ ■

The next morning I was up at dawn, all too aware that this was our most critical day. When I reached the Portman Hotel, I went straight to Wu's room, where I found him pacing the floor in a natty double-breasted pinstriped suit that made him look like a costumed actor who had just wandered off a film set re-creating the Shanghai French Concession in the 1930s.

A knock on the door made us both jump. However, it was only Gelber, who was equally jumpy.

Finally, it was time for Wu to go down to the lobby, meet the prison officials, and squire them up to the special suite where Lloyd had set up three hidden cameras.

"Good luck!" I said, giving Wu a farewell clasp.

Gelber and I were now left alone, both of us feeling a little as if we were in a hospital waiting room apprehensively awaiting word from an operating theater about the success or failure of a complex surgery. The time ticked by painfully slowly. But, at 11:30 a.m. the phone came to life. It was Bradley.

"I'm out," Bradley announced with no suggestion of emotion.

"How did it go?" Gelber asked.

"Fine, just fine," Bradley replied, his calmness now wonderfully reassuring. "Wu's downstairs with them for lunch."

Then came a knock on the door. I cracked it open without removing the safety chain. Lloyd was outside with his three briefcases.

"Everything go OK?" asked Gelber anxiously, as soon as Lloyd got inside.

"Just great," Lloyd replied with a broad grin. "But Bradley scared us to death by coming in without his remote microphone on!" Lloyd gave a nervous laugh. "When we figured out what was wrong, we had to bullshit the comrades about Bradley needing to rush back to his room for an urgent phone call from headquarters. However, when he finally returned and got going, he was great! He almost convinced me he was a company chief!"

As Lloyd previewed a few clips from one of the cameras, we were all relieved to see that this time there had been no apparent equipment malfunctions.

"Because we want a long-term relationship, we have to be sure about the reliability of the work," we saw Bradley intone to the prison factory managers. Then turning to Wu, he pointedly asked, "Harry, have you visited their factory?"

"No, I haven't," Wu replied earnestly. "I only visited their manager in his office."

"You have to visit their workshop!" insisted Bradley. "Because according to our company policy, we must see the workshop before we can place a large order."

"So, what you're saying is, if we cannot get a factory visit, we may not be able to implement the contract?" deadpanned Wu. Bradley nodded.

We were interrupted by Wu calling from the downstairs hotel restaurant where he and the prison officials were lunching and discussing this very topic.

"They really want to do business with us!" said Wu, his voice hoarse with excitement. "However, they say they can't let anyone into the factory without permission from higher-ups at the Shanghai Reform-Through-Labor Bureau. They've been calling and calling their office, but haven't yet gotten through. They keep apologizing and saying, 'Well, maybe tomorrow.' But I told them, 'No! Tomorrow won't work. We're leaving tonight!'"

Lloyd was sitting amidst a tangle of wires, cameras, and monitors, making copies of some of the tapes he had just shot so we would have dupes of some of the originals. But since it would take several hours to copy all the tapes from the three cameras, he, Bradley, and Gelber were trying to identify only the most important sections. Then I was responsible for getting them to Hong Kong. But, because I did not dare take our tape cassettes through Chinese customs myself, I had to run them to another hotel and hand them off to a "pigeon" we had laid on to fly them to Hong Kong before I independently arrived to pick them up.

The phone rang.

"The prison officials can't reach their boss, so I don't think I'll get into the factory today," reported Wu. "I've told them that I'll try to convince my boss to make the deal anyway."

We were all disappointed by the news but agreed it was far too dangerous to linger here in Shanghai another day.

As Lloyd and Gelber continued copying, I called our pigeon. She was standing by in the lobby of her hotel. Making matters even more tense for me was the fact that my own flight to Hong Kong left in several hours. If all went perfectly, I would have just enough time to hand off the tapes, bolt to the airport, and make my own flight.

The minutes went by like hours, but finally Lloyd stood up, wiped his brow, stuffed some cassettes into an envelope, and handed them to me. I dashed out the door with my suitcase.

Once I reached our pigeon's hotel, I ran into the lobby and, like a relay racer handing off a baton, passed her the envelope, asked her to call me as soon as she got to Hong Kong, jumped back into my taxi, and sped to Hongqiao Airport.

My very last wicket was Chinese emigration. When I handed my passport to the uniformed customs officer, he studied it with a concentration that was frightening. But then he raised his exit chop and, as if he were a judge pronouncing "Case Closed!," brought it resolutely down on my visa.

Chapter Seventeen

MISSION ACCOMPLISHED

AS SOON AS I WOKE the next morning in Hong Kong, I felt intoxicated with relief and immediately called Baifang. She, too, was relieved to know that I was safely back.

"I have some other good news," she announced. "The obstetrician says our baby will probably be late."

Heaving a sigh of relief, I told her I would wait for Gelber, Bradley, and the crew to arrive back in Hong Kong from Beijing and then come straight home.

After we hung up, I ordered a full English breakfast from room service in celebration. As I ate while reading the *South China Morning Post* and gazing out across Hong Kong Harbor, the certainty that here, at least, no police would come crashing through the door allowed me to drop my guard for the first time in months. Rarely have I enjoyed a meal more!

However, while I was out of China Wu, Gelber, Bradley, and the CBS crew were not. In fact, just then they were scheduled to be trying to penetrate the Qinghe Farm prison complex outside Tianjin. After breakfast, I began looking through the book manuscript Wu had been working on about his life, which he had left here in Hong Kong for safekeeping before he entered China. I quickly found the section he had written about his years at Qinghe. His first imprisonment there was during the Great Leap Forward, the "three difficult years" (三年灾害)—from 1959 to 1962—when Mao's communization of agriculture had led to a mass famine that killed upwards of forty million people across China. Before it was over, Wu himself had been reduced to a skeletal seventy-two pounds in Qinghe. He wrote that his fellow inmates "no longer looked human, but like some other kind of creature, or ghosts." He described the breathing of living prisoners as "so weak that it made almost no noise. By only one sign did we know that a fellow prisoner had died; when he failed to sit up at mealtime."

I was startled when my room phone rang. It was Wu himself.

"It's over," he announced.

"What do you mean?"

"We drove right into Qinghe!" he laughed with brio. "We even managed to buy some peaches and grapes for Bradley from a couple of prison guards along the road by a vineyard that grows grapes for Remy Martin in France to make Dynasty wine!"

As I had come to know Wu better, I had learned that when things went well, he easily forgot security concerns. Now he sounded so full of relief and pride that, despite still being in China and in jeopardy, he could not resist announcing his successes.

"Good news," I responded. "When do you leave?"

"I fly back to Hong Kong tomorrow, and . . . "

"Let's talk further then," I interjected, not wanting him to divulge any more incriminating information over the phone.

"OK," he agreed.

■ ■ ■

That evening members of the pro-democracy Hong Kong Alliance were staging a candlelight rally in solidarity with Chinese political prisoners, so I decided to go and have a look. These mostly young, earnest protesters demonstrating in support of their mainland colleagues were a reminder of how closely linked Hong Kong's future now was to Beijing's. Already the CCP evinced little tolerance for the colony being used as what PRC propagandists called "a counterrevolutionary base to subvert socialism in China" (一个旨在颠覆中国社会主义制度的反革命基地). How Beijing would respond after Hong Kong reverted from British to Chinese rule in 1997 was anyone's guess. Despite Deng's promise of fifty years of autonomy, it was difficult to imagine that the CCP would continue tolerating the kinds of indignities against its one-party rule represented by this demonstration.

When I got back to my hotel room, the message light on my phone was blinking. Our pigeon had called. An hour later, she arrived and handed off the tapes from Shanghai, the improbable harvest of our eight-month-long effort. The fact that in the end things had fallen into place seemed nothing short of miraculous. Now only two things remained undone: Bradley and Gelber had to wrap up their interviews with Chinese trade officials in Beijing and get back to Hong Kong with the crew and their new interviews. And Wu, too, had to make it safely out of China.

■ ■ ■

With butterflies in my stomach, I boarded the Star Ferry to Kowloon and grabbed a taxi to Kai Tak Airport, where Wu was scheduled to land that night. Once at the terminal, I kept monitoring the arrivals board. When it suddenly showed his Tianjin flight as having landed, my heart jumped. But when twenty, then forty-five minutes passed and he had not emerged from the customs area, I began to worry. We had somehow gotten through so many other uncertainties, it would be an unthinkable tragedy if something untoward happened now at this penultimate moment of our long and uncertain odyssey. Might Chinese authorities have prevented him from boarding his plane? Once again, I found myself besieged with a host of terrifying possibilities.

"Are you coming from Tianjin," I anxiously asked a Chinese woman with a small child who had an Air China baggage tag flopping from her suitcase handle.

"Yes," she smiled as her child looked up quizzically at a foreigner speaking Mandarin.

Another five minutes passed. Still no sign of Wu.

Then a throng of passengers exited from a flight that had landed from Jakarta long after Wu's. Just when I had yearned to be able to declare final victory, I found myself once again waiting and beset by deepening worries.

Then . . . there he was! He wore a black Tibetan cowboy hat from Qinghai and was pushing a luggage cart from which the horns of his Mongolian gazelle sprung, making him look like any other tourist coming home from a holiday.

"Welcome back, Comrade," I said, embracing him.

"Jesus!" he exclaimed. "We did it!"

As we drove back to the hotel, he regaled me with details of their expedition into the Qinghe Farm.

"When we arrived from Shanghai at Tianjin Airport, the van and driver I'd reserved didn't show up," he began. "I'd planned to drive the van to Qinghe myself the next morning, so we wouldn't have to worry about a driver getting suspicious. However, I couldn't now just flag down a cab and ask some guy to take us and all our camera gear into a prison camp! So, the next morning I got up at dawn, went down to the train station, and chatted with a bunch of drivers waiting for customers. Finally, I found a guy with a van whom I felt I could trust . . . if I paid him enough!

"After we picked up Gelber, Bradley, and the crew and were headed to the prison farm, I began kidding the driver about how these foreigners just wanted to see a really big and impressive Chinese farm. And it seemed quite natural to him, because most ordinary Chinese tend to view foreigners as having strange desires anyway." He gave a hearty laugh. "But then, when we arrived at the Yongding River Bridge on the edge of the sprawling camp, we were stopped at a guardhouse by armed police."

"So what happened?"

"Well, I think the guards just thought that the CBS crew was a bunch of foreign engineers or something," he explained.

"Anyway, they were so unconcerned, they even shared a few cans of soda with us and posed for some snapshots!"

"And no one became suspicious?"

"No one!" he replied triumphantly.

"I thought these camps were so security conscious no outsiders could get near them."

"You know," Wu replied reflectively, "I don't think those guards could even imagine an unauthorized group of foreign journalists like us trying anything like this!"

"But a six-foot-tall Black American television news anchor with a bunch of white TV producers and a crew with huge cameras? Wouldn't that arouse suspicion?"

"Yeah, I know it sounds crazy," he responded. "But you have to understand how provincial Chinese in out-of-the-way places think. When they see a foreigner, their first assumption is that they must have a reason and official approval to be there. They can't imagine it any other way."

"What was it like to be back in your old prison camp yourself?" I asked, changing direction.

"Oh God! It pulled up lots of memories!" He shook his head. "Now, I just need some time to digest it all."

And now he would have that time. He would fly the next day to Taiwan, where his anxious wife awaited him.

▪ ▪ ▪

That evening Gelber called from Beijing. The crew had met their handlers from the Ministry of Radio, Film, and

Television, and as far anyone could tell, they were none the wiser about the excursion into the Qinghe Farm camp with Wu.

"And what about your tour there?" I asked.

"To be honest, I was scared shitless!" Gelber responded in a winsomely unheroic way. "I mean, think about it: We just drove a goddamn van tooled up with CBS video cameras right into a reform-through-labor camp and got away with it!"

"What kind of footage did you get?"

"I think we got some pretty good stuff. And here in Beijing we shot several really good interviews with trade officials."

Because he was talking so openly from Beijing, I assumed he was speaking on a secure line. However, I did not want to ask him directly. Once again I realized how lousy we Americans were at exercising political caution and restraining our speech. We were just not accustomed to having to be mindful about what we said, because for us it rarely had dire consequences.

"And some other good news!" I added. "Our tapes from Shanghai and Wu have both arrived safely in Hong Kong."

"Fantastic!" riposted Gelber. "Why don't you have a quick look at some of the tapes?"

Ever mindful of the disappointments from our first trip, neither of us was quite ready to proclaim victory.

■ ■ ■

With a typhoon closing in on Hong Kong, I rented a video player and hunkered down in my hotel room to screen the Shanghai tapes.

The three briefcase cameras seemed to have functioned without a hitch in Shanghai. There were Wu and the Chinese prison officials negotiating "the deal." And there was Bradley striding like a corporate god into the special hotel suite. With impeccable executive authority he greeted the Chinese prison officials and with a disarming innocence asked how illegal prison-made goods were exported abroad. And the answers these officials gave were incredibly incriminating. But from the perspective of television, what was even more incriminating was the fact that we had captured video images of these prison officials sitting with their tool catalogues open before them eagerly peddling wrenches and pliers to people they believed were U.S. buyers.

Then, with Wu translating, Bradley deftly raised the question of forced labor, asking the prison factory chief if he foresaw any problems doing business because of U.S. laws. As the chief stepped unknowingly into Bradley's trap, I found myself feeling a little sorry for him. Yes, he worked at a prison facility that used forced laborers. Yes, prisoners were doubtless mistreated and exploited. And yes, some of these prison factory workers were undoubtedly political prisoners! However, the two officials looked all too human and mortal in this video. Just as Wu had lamented to me several months before, these men were just ordinary guys with ordinary lives and ordinary families trying to do the jobs they had been assigned to by the state. And here a cabal of Americans ensconced in a luxury hotel had sneaked into their country and right into their midst to entrap them in ways they had doubtless never imagined even in their most paranoid fantasies. And in China, that's saying a lot!

Of course, I knew full well how much misery China's prison system had inflicted on countless millions of innocent people like Wu. But it was still impossible to ignore the reality that when our *60 Minutes* segment aired, it would be these guys, not their superiors, who would get blamed, punished, and maybe even locked up.

Next I turned to the tapes that Wu had shot in Shanxi, Gansu, and Qinghai. Much of it was still infuriatingly jumpy and unfocused with many herky-jerky sequences where it was impossible to discern what was happening. And there were shots of the sky embellished with sounds of panting and urgently whispering voices when Wu forgot to turn off the camera as he hurried away.

"Careful! They're looking! Let's go!" someone said as the camera careened around.

But there were also a number of steadier sequences. He had captured a great shot showing lines of blue uniformed prisoners marching down a road in what looked like Qinghai. A second sequence showed a prisoner at the Qinghai Hide and Garment Plant (the Qinghai No. 2 Reform-Through-Labor Detachment) wading chest-deep in a giant vat of toxic tanning chemicals. A third showed inmates with sledgehammers at Tanggemu Prison (Qinghai No. 13 Reform-Through-Labor Detachment) clearing away rubble from a collapsed structure that looked as if it had been hit by an earthquake.

Finally came a long, languid shot as Wu walked down Nanshan Road in Qinghai's provincial capital, Xining, where prison factories run by the province's Reform-Through-Labor Bureau had set up outlets to market their wares to local consumers. As

Wu's hidden camera panned around this peaceful tree-lined street, probing signs hanging over each prison enterprise, unperturbed pedestrians with shopping bags strolled calmly by. It was a chilling display of just how routinized reform-through-labor institutions had become in everyday Qinghai life.

One other riveting sequence showed two managers of the Qinghai Hide and Garment Factory. One, dressed in civilian clothes, introduced himself as Chief Gao Hongzhou, and the other, attired in a khaki police uniform with four gold stripes on the cuffs, was introduced as Manager Wan Xiaohua. Both proudly riffed about the $5 million in annual foreign exports their prison enterprise had laundered last year through a Hong Kong trading company called Winmate. As in Shanghai, these Qinghai prison entrepreneurs appeared only too eager to do business with anyone, including Americans, even though they understood they would be breaking American law.

"Let me make something clear between us, now that you've seen the factory," said chain-smoking Chief Gao from behind an impressive executive desk. You don't need . . . "

"Things are very clear to me!" interrupted Wu. "We in the U.S. are aware of Congress and all that."

"But let me explain," persisted Gao. "In the U.S., they have their own laws, and they are out to impose those laws on China."

"Well, that's their concern," demurred Wu, as a uniformed prisoner with a shaved head appeared in-frame to serve tea like a house slave on a plantation in the American South.

"In this factory we make our own decisions," continued Manager Wan emphatically. "When it comes to exports, we'll take the responsibility for finding an export company."

Then they tried to convince Wu to invest $500,000 worth of foreign-made equipment in their factory, proposing to pay him back by shipping finished hides to the United States.

But the crowning moment of Wu's visit to this far-flung prison factory came when Chief Gao and Manager Wan spontaneously began discussing the "sock incident" involving U.S. Rep. Frank Wolf's congressional visit to Beijing #1 Prison, where stockings imprinted in English for export had been spotted by members of the U.S. Congress. As Chief Gao told it, following Rep. Wolf's prison visit the Ministry of Justice distributed a document instructing prison factory managers how best to explain the incident to outsiders if questioned.

"Oh, yeah, the 'sock incident!' " Manager Wan voluntarily piped up. "We hear it caused a storm in the U.S.!"

"I hadn't heard that," responded Wu, feigning ignorance in hopes of getting them to say more.

"It was in the U.S. Congress over giving China most favored nation status," explained Chief Gao, smiling slyly. "It caused a lot of controversy. But from the perspective of what we want to do . . ."

"I just want to buy your products," soothed Wu. "And instead of paying cash, I'll buy you equipment."

"Oh, yes. That'll be good!" grinned Chief Gao.

"I've talked to Mr. Wan about setting prices and about how you'll find an export-import company for us," continued Wu. "But I don't want to pay extra to this company."

"We can either ask the China Export-Import Corporation in Canton or the Qinghai Xushan company to represent us," offered Manager Wan obligingly.

Then, as Wu was being guided on a tour of the prison factory showroom, he spotted a wall banner from the Ministry of Justice commending the prison as "An Advanced Unit for Repressing Rebellions and Cleansing Chaos." This was a national award given to the prison for its help in "suppressing turmoil," which was Party jargon for putting down the pro-democracy demonstrations that swept China during the spring of 1989.

Besides this revealing banner, Wu spotted another damning piece of visual evidence: a framed 1988 certificate from the Ministry of Foreign Economic Relations and Trade (MOFERT) explicitly granting the prison factory export rights.

Wu's next cassette showed Qinghai's infamous Tanggemu Camp (the Qinghai #13 Reform-Through-Labor Detachment), where the well-known democracy dissident Wei Jingsheng had been imprisoned for four years. Astonishingly, Wu infiltrated it by dressing up in a Public Security Bureau uniform and posing as a visiting official.

Finally, came a sequence showing a large workshop at the Lanzhou Motor Coach Plant (Gansu No. 3 Reform-Through-Labor Detachment) where buses were being assembled by prisoners with shaved heads.

As these images flickered on screen, it was clear that this time Wu had more than fulfilled his mission.

Chapter Eighteen

BEIJING SENSITIVITIES

"BRADLEY JUST DID a fantastic interview with this vice minister of foreign relations and trade," effused Gelber when he called from Beijing. "This guy just lied through his teeth! We couldn't have gotten a more repellent bureaucrat, if we'd ordered him from central casting."

While I was glad to hear Bradley's interviews had gone well, I was alarmed by Gelber's absence of caution in speaking over what I assumed was a hotel room phone. Yes, we were very near the end of our saga, but Gelber, Bradley, and the CBS crew were still in China. Gelber was referring to the interview Bradley had just done with the vice minister of the Ministry of Foreign Economic Relations and Trade, Tong Zhiguang. Tong spoke excellent English and was just about to lead a delegation to the United States to iron out controversies over pirated intellectual property, unfair trade barriers, and exports made with forced labor, all issues that were bedeviling U.S.-China relations.

Gelber told me that Bradley had started off by telling Vice Minister Tong that Americans, including many members of Congress, were deeply upset by the way Chinese troops had fired on unarmed demonstrators in 1989 and the fact that many of those protesters were still in Chinese prisons, possibly making products for export to the United States.

"The transcript will provide some of the most damning moments for our program," promised Gelber.

One example came about when Bradley asked Tong, "Can you understand that Americans don't want products made by these people under forced labor exported to the United States?"

"As a matter of policy, the Chinese government never allows the export of what you call 'forced labor' products," Tong smugly rejoined. "This has been the policy and it will remain the policy of the Chinese government. . . . [However, since] there are many trading companies in China, a few pieces of such products just might have leaked out."

"You know, I have to be honest with you, Mr. Tong," Bradley countered, ready to spring one of those traps for which *60 Minutes* had become renowned. "I've spoken to officials in Shanghai at the Laodong Machinery Plant, which uses forced labor. They said that they don't export directly [but] do it through export-import companies."

"It's not to my knowledge," responded Tong evasively. "We do have prisoners producing products in China . . . [but] no present related manufacturing facilities have ever been given the right to engage in foreign trade. They're not allowed."

"So, how is it they're able to do it?" persisted Bradley, his voice dripping with righteousness.

"Nobody knows," answered Tong, his smugness beginning to be tinged by new uncertainty. "But I'm not saying it must have happened."

"But there it is. Right in the middle of Shanghai," pressed Bradley, waving an offending letter from the company as if he were a prosecuting attorney in a trial.

"To me it's inconceivable," spluttered Tong. "If that's true, they are violating Chinese policy. . . . The Chinese government never allows what you call 'forced labor products.' "

"You think this is a mistake?"

"It's either a mistake or the letter is in doubt," responded the rattled vice minister.

"It's in print!" insisted Bradley.

"I never know," responded Tong.

"Frankly, it's hard, based on what we've seen, to conclude that people in this country are being honest with us about the exportation of products from forced labor," continued Bradley, no longer looking right at Tong, but into the camera as if to address the twenty million Americans viewers he knew would be watching this *60 Minutes* program.

"We are very honest," responded Tong, becoming incensed. "I'm telling you nothing but the truth!"

"President Bush, for example, wrote to a United States senator [Sen. Max Baucus from Montana] saying that we have obtained a firm high-level commitment to prevent the sale of prison labor products to the U.S.," continued Bradley.

"That is true."

"Now, there are people in the U.S. Congress who are saying that our president has been fooled."

"No, he's not," parried Tong unconvincingly.

"So, the policy of your government is not to export forced labor products?"

"No, not at all. "

"And China is able to enforce that, to ensure that it doesn't happen anymore?"

"We have no doubt about that."

"And the incidents I found in Shanghai . . . just leaked through?"

"I can only say that they [Chinese government officials] are firm in enforcing the policy today."

"Was there a particular date when this firmness took place, when the government said, 'From this day on that it will have a firm policy, and this will not be allowed?' " Bradley persevered somewhat facetiously.

"I can't quote a particular date. It has been my impression that the Chinese government is getting firmer and firmer in that particular respect in the last two years in particular." After an awkward pause, he added, "That doesn't mean to say the government wasn't firm before. [But] it's getting firmer now. . . . People there [in the U.S.] tend to put so many unrelated issues together to bear upon most favored nation status (MFN), including human rights, arms control, forced labor . . . "

"So, continuing China's most favored nation trade status should have nothing to do with human rights in this country?" Bradley archly countered.

"No."

"It's only about business?"

"Business is business!" said Tong with finality.

As he sanctimoniously intoned "Business is business," I could hear the *60 Minutes* stopwatch begin ticking to signal the end of another successful takedown.

"The guy just fell apart!" exclaimed Gelber. "He really didn't know how to reply!" Then Gelber added, "What I don't understand: Are these guys really ignorant about what's going on under their noses, or do they just think they can bullshit us as foreigners?"

Chapter Nineteen

AN END AND A BEGINNING

AS I ENTERED the lobby of the Mandarin Oriental Hotel, I was summoned to the front desk and handed a note:

> Would you kindly contact me as soon as possible?
> Yours truly, The Assistant Manager

Yes, I was in Hong Kong under British common law, not in Beijing under the "dictatorship of the proletariat." Nonetheless this summons was reminiscent enough of the one I had received in Beijing from the Palace Hotel's front desk to alarm me:

What had I done now?

Had the crew run into trouble in Beijing?

I finally found the morning-coated British assistant manager.

"Ah, yes," he flushed when I told him my name. "Well . . . we've just received a call."

"From where?" I inquired anxiously.

"From San Francisco," he stammered. "And . . . well, your wife has just gone into labor and left for the hospital with a friend. Perhaps our concierge can help you book a flight home."

I stood thunderstruck in the middle of the lobby as other guests swept past. Our baby was almost a month early and Baifang had not even finished her childbirth classes!

Reeling, I dashed upstairs to my room to call the hospital. Then . . . suddenly I was talking with her. She was in the labor room, groggy, but stoic as ever. Our two friends assured me that everything was going normally.

After I hung up, I tried to collect myself. More than anything I want to be by her side. However, even if I left Hong Kong immediately, there was no way I could arrive in San Francisco in time for the birth.

Two hours later I called the hospital again. When Baifang miraculously came on the line, she reported that they were about to wheel her into the delivery room. I sent hugs, sat down on the bed, and gazed out across Hong Kong Harbor. However, in my mind I was on the other side of the Pacific Ocean with the woman who was my wife, my partner in almost everything, and the love of my life.

Several hours later, my room phone rang. It was one of our friends in the delivery room with Baifang.

"Congratulations! You have a son!" she exclaimed. Baifang was heroic and is doing fine."

Before one great undertaking had ended, another had begun. I was just trying to absorb all this when the phone rang again.

"I've just got to tell ya, we've really nailed this!" a voice exploded. It was Gelber.

"You're back!" I exclaimed.

"Yeah! Just arrived. Let's have dinner!"

"Great! But . . . I have a son!"

"A son? Way to go! We've a lot to celebrate!"

Moments later Wu, just back from Taipei himself, appeared at the door, making our hotel feel like an aircraft carrier with fighter planes landing one after the other safely back on the flight deck after a dangerous mission.

At dinner a grinning Gelber proposed a toast to my new son and the success of our project. Then, after a brief pause, he turned to Wu.

"Hey, I was just thinking of those agents you told us about who worked for that company in Qinghai that sold yak hides? Didn't you say they had an office here in Hong Kong? Could we visit them?"

Wu stared down at his plate for a moment, then sprang up and went to the cashier's desk. A few moments later he returned with a Hong Kong phone book.

"Here it is," he announced triumphantly. "The Winmate Trading Co., Wah Hing Commercial Centre, Yau Ma Tei."

"Bingo!" said Gelber with a huge smile. "Fire up the lipstick cameras for one more round!"

As Wu ran to use the phone, Gelber turned to me.

"And Bradley wants to interview you tomorrow morning before you go. After that we're done, I promise!"

Having taken the project this far, and after being reassured by my friends in the hospital with Baifang that everything was fine, I decided to delay my return home one more day.

It had been a long, uncertain process, and I was amazed we had gotten this far without anyone being detained. Wu had finished an important piece of his life's work. Gelber had steered our project through some very treacherous shoals. And, me . . . ? Well, after eight months on this unlikely odyssey, I could hardly wait to get home to my wife and new child!

■ ■ ■

After hardly sleeping, I jolted awake, grabbed a quick breakfast, and did my interview with Bradley. I used the occasion to emphasize that what distinguished China's prison system from others elsewhere was that it not only extrajudicially detained and held untold numbers of political prisoners, but often compelled them to labor involuntarily for the very state that had so arbitrarily incarcerated them.

As we were finishing the interview, Wu appeared.

"I got them!" he proclaimed jubilantly.

"Got who?" asked Gelber.

"Winmate, and they've agreed to meet with us."

So, with Wu again acting the role of a Chinese American businessman and Norman Lloyd now playing his corporate retainer, but also toting a camera hidden in a briefcase, they set off for Winmate's office. There they were cordially received by

Manager Samuel Poon and Assistant Manager Linda Li, who both readily acknowledged that their client in Qinghai was a prison camp and that they frequently visited it as its exclusive Hong Kong agent. In fact, they proudly announced, in 1990 they had done $3.5 million in business with the prison and in the coming year expected the figure to climb to $5.2 million.

The Winmate execs also revealed something else that was intriguing: Seventy percent of all their Qinghai-sourced leather was exported from Hong Kong to South Korea for processing into jackets and other finished goods before being transshipped to the United States and elsewhere around the world. In other words, Hong Kong was serving as an entrepot and laundry machine for leather tanned with forced labor in China that was then shipped to Korea for processing into finished goods destined to be sold with ROK labels in the United States and other countries. For all American buyers, customs agents, and consumers could tell, these products came from the Republic of Korea.

These revelations cast a new shadow on Hong Kong, which lobbyists besieging Washington had been claiming would be unnecessarily and unjustly hurt by denying China MFN status. As it turned out, Hong Kong was in the prison labor supply chain, too, and profiting from it by laundering raw materials.

As the CBS crew were returning from their Winmate interview, Wu asked if he could take a quick look at the tapes they had just shot to make sure all had gone well. To everyone's horror, they discovered Lloyd's hidden camera had somehow malfunctioned, leaving only blank tape.

Once again Wu refused to accept defeat. He immediately phoned Manager Poon, told him his big boss had unexpectedly just become free and would like to personally invite him and Linda Li to the Mandarin Oriental Hotel for a special visit. They agreed to come right over.

Ed Bradley was still in Hong Kong, but because *60 Minu*tes was regularly broadcast in the colony, we all feared that if he masqueraded again as CEO, someone might recognize him. Instead, Gelber decided to dress soundman Ned Hall up in a suit and tie and deputize him to play Wu's "big American boss."

When the two unknowing Winmate agents arrived at the hotel, Wu squired them upstairs to another special suite where the now tested and retested lipstick cameras had been set up in briefcases placed in strategic places to secretly document the meeting.

The highlight of the negotiation came when, feigning naivete, Hall asked Poon and Li, "Are the laborers themselves prisoners?"

"Yes," replied Poon matter-of-factly.

"Have you had experience with this kind of labor in the past, and have you found it to be dependable?" pressed Hall.

"Yes," affirmed Li. "They have their own regulations. And we send our people to keep checking the quality. If we report to them that the quality is not up to standard, the prisoners will have punishment of beatings, or some other things."

Once again, I could hear the *60 Minutes* stopwatch clicking out another successful takedown.

■ ■ ■

Now I was free to go home!

Thirteen hours after boarding my flight in Hong Kong, I landed in San Francisco and went directly to the hospital. There was my weary, smiling wife holding a small, pink homunculus in her arms. We named him Jonathan Sebastian Schell after my younger brother, Jonathan, and Johann Sebastian Bach. For his Chinese name, we chose Baifang's last name, *Liu* 刘 and my Chinese last name Xia 夏, plus the character for the Qing Dynasty 清, meaning "clear." With 刘夏清's birth, another great chapter of my life with Baifang began.

Part IV

WHY THIS STORY STILL MATTERS

Chapter Twenty

HOME FREE

WHEN THE CBS CREW finally got back to New York, there was much rejoicing at *60 Minutes*. But to bring this costly and difficult project fully to term, Gelber and his editors still had to take the hours of material we had shot and transform it all into a short, pithy, dramatic television story. As they worked, the debate over whether China should be accorded permanent MFN trade status heated up in Washington, D.C. With the Beijing Massacre only two years past, the memory of that nightmarish time still agitated many U.S. congressional representatives. So, even though President Bush supported an extension, there was substantial reluctance to extend carte blanche trade privileges to China.

After almost a year of work, "Made in China" aired in the fall of 1991. *Newsweek* ran a cover story; the *Washington Post*, *Business Week*, the *World Journal*, the BBC, the Voice of America, and many other media outlets extensively covered the story. Senate Majority Leader George Mitchell asked for a meeting, and a congressional committee announced its intention to hold hearings on products made with prison labor.

Beijing's reaction to having its darkest interstices exposed by an American television network was predictable. Wu Jianmin, China's Foreign Ministry spokesman, charged *60 Minutes* with having "confounded black and white" and attacked the program as "notorious for vilifying China" and for revealing its "extreme hatred for the social system which the Chinese people have chosen."

Despite Beijing's criticisms, the program went on to win an Emmy, an Alfred I. duPont–Columbia University Silver Baton award, and other plaudits. However, despite all the publicity the program generated, Beijing was still granted unconditional MFN trade status. Evidently many in Washington, including President Bush, continued hoping that more engagement would somehow encourage China's leaders into accepting a closer and more open relationship with the United States and the world. Soon the Clinton administration, which came into office in 1993, was paving the way for China to be admitted into the World Trade Organization as well. When it formally gained accession in 2001, President Clinton himself justified U.S. support this way.

"It will not create a free society in China overnight or guarantee that China will play by global rules," he acknowledged. However, he insisted, "over time, I believe it will move China faster and further in the right direction, and certainly will do that more than rejection. So, if you believe in a future of greater openness and freedom for the people of China, you ought to be for this agreement. If you believe in a future of greater prosperity for the American people, you certainly should be for this agreement."

■ ■ ■

It was only after our program finally aired that I began leafing through the journal I had kept throughout the project. Already it seemed like a tall tale that might have happened to someone else, or something I had perhaps just dreamed or seen in a film. But by the time I had finished reading what I had written, I was wondering if others might not find our saga a way to get inside China through an unusual portal. So, I set to work editing the journal and then sent the draft off to my editor at *The New Yorker*.

But by the time a reedited version came back, I had gained enough distance from the whole project to realize that if a detailed account of this *60 Minutes* program's origins and evolution came out under my name in a magazine like *The New Yorker*, the consequences for me, our family, and our friends in China would be dire. While I had not been prominently featured on camera in the program, this first-person narrative describing my role in the planning of the whole venture would most certainly attract Beijing's attention and elicit a punitive response. One thing was certain: There was no way that the Chinese Communist Party would view what we had done as a legitimate piece of investigative journalism.

As an independent writer who wanted to continue chronicling China's development and who supported his family by doing so, I needed to be able to travel there. But this very personalized account would put that access in grave jeopardy, right at the time when I had become not only a husband but a new father, with a multigenerational family largely dependent on me for support.

After no small amount of torment, with great reluctance I informed my editor at *The New Yorker* that I intended to withdraw the piece from publication. Then I dropped the manuscript into a box, put the box on a closet shelf, and there it slumbered undisturbed for the next three decades as I went about other projects, many of which did, in fact, depend on my ability to return to China.

After the *60 Minutes* program aired, Wu was widely celebrated and went on to work on several other equally risky projects. In 1994, he began a collaboration with the BBC that saw him sally forth to Xinjiang, China's westernmost province, which *The Xinjiang Legal Journal* described as a place "where the 'reform-through-labor *laogai*' industry plays a comparatively important role." Wu described it more bluntly as "another subjugated region that was fast becoming the home base of the *laogai* industry."

By that time, Wu had gained American citizenship and a U.S. passport. He had also undergone yet another name change, giving him an important new safeguard against Chinese oversight. With an American passport now identifying him as Peter H. Wu, he flew to Kazakhstan and headed for its border with Xinjiang, where he managed to slip through Chinese immigration screening back into China.

After penetrating a number of *laogai* camps in Xinjiang, Wu also began investigating China's organ transplant business, which was reportedly selling human organs harvested from executed prisoners to wealthy recipients, some from foreign countries. The BBC documentary that resulted made him an even better known crusader against rights abuses among Chinese prisoners.

In 1995, Wu set off on yet another investigative project in Xinjiang, this one into the shadowy Xinjiang Production and Construction Corporation (新疆生产建设兵团), a quasi-military organization known in short as the *bingtuan* (兵团), or Military Unit. For decades this network of camps operated a whole host of agricultural and industrial enterprises in the province. These camps, originally constructed in the 1950s to "develop and guard the border areas" by resettling soldiers in the region, soon ended up harboring tens of thousands of political prisoners.

It was in one of these camps, at Shihezi (石河子), some ninety miles from the provincial capital, Urumqi, that the Chinese artist Ai Weiwei spent much of his early life with his father, Ai Qing, China's most renowned twentieth-century poet. During one of Mao's mass political movements, the Anti-Rightist Campaign (反右运动) that lasted from 1957 to 1959, Ai Qing was labeled a "rightist" (右派) and unceremoniously banished from Beijing, first to Heilongjiang Province in northern Manchuria and then to a *bingtuan* in Xinjiang Province, where everyone was, in effect, a forced laborer.

By 1995, the World Bank had committed some $23 billion in loans to China, and Xinjiang was one of the bank's largest recipients. Wu wanted to investigate how much of these funds had been assigned to *bingtuan* facilities. So on June 19, 1995, he set off on a third clandestine trip, again attempting to enter

Xinjiang from Kazakhstan. This time, however, despite his new American passport, Wu was identified at the Chinese border by customs agents, detained, flown from Xinjiang to the central Chinese city of Wuhan, and imprisoned. His situation looked bleak.

However, since he was now a U.S. citizen, American diplomats were able to visit him once a month. With his wife working the media back home, and even First Lady Hillary Clinton, former National Security Council director Henry Kissinger, and Assistant Secretary of State Winston Lord all weighing in on his behalf in Washington, an arrangement to get him released was finally worked out, but only after the Chinese government conducted a trial. At this trial, Wu was found guilty of committing "grave offenses," including spying and stealing state secrets, and sentenced to fifteen years in prison. However, the Party artfully tacked on a "supplementary penalty" to his sentence: expulsion from China. Thus the Chinese government was able to use this sleight of hand to both find Wu guilty and off-load him to the United States, thereby avoiding another serious diplomatic crisis.

To get released, Wu had to admit to "damaging the interest of the Chinese government" and "violating Chinese law" as well as to sign a statement saying, "I keenly regret and feel remorse for the consequences of what I have done." Wu consented to make these admissions on the advice of American diplomats, who believed that such a confession would allow China to save enough face to release him.

However, this arrangement did not prevent Wu from retracting his confession as soon as he was safely outside China. And that is exactly what he did.

"They knew I was lying, and I knew that they knew," Wu defiantly declared upon arriving back in the United States. "But they had no problem making a deal with someone they knew was lying. That's how their system works."

Wu was given a hero's welcome, and his life quickly became a whirlwind of articles, speeches, media appearances, and testimonials at U.S. congressional hearings. He also continued to work through his Laogai (Reform-Through-Labor) Research Foundation and wrote two more books, including *Bitter Winds: A Memoir of My Years in China's Gulag*, published in 1994, and *Troublemaker: One Man's Crusade Against China's Cruelty*, published in 1996.

So, how should Wu Hongda's life and efforts be assessed?

In describing Wu's written work in the *New York Review of Books*, the eminent Yale University historian of China, Jonathan Spence, wrote: "In the end, after all the words, deaths, and suffering, it is Harry Wu who most strongly bears witness by having the courage to go back to the camps where he had endured so much. After Harry emigrated to America, he wanted to return to take photographs of the labor camps to accompany his factual account. He did this not only to 'speak bitterness,' as the Chinese Communists liked to say in their heyday, but to awaken the conscience of people in Western countries who buy prison-made goods."

When Wu died in 2016, at seventy-nine, I felt a sense of loss. For almost a year, we had worked closely together. And, as Spence observed, despite all that he had endured during Mao's revolution, he still managed maintain a sense of right and wrong and to resist the indignities of political imprisonment in China.

Unfortunately, before he passed away, his human rights legacy became tarnished by accusations of sexual misconduct and the mishandling of a fund that had been entrusted to his management because of all the worthy work he had done to disclose the abuses of China's reform-through labor system.

The accusation of financial wrongdoing came out of a complex settlement with Yahoo after its Chinese corporate arm disclosed data to the CCP on the activities of a Chinese newspaper editor and PEN member, Shi Tao, and several other dissidents. Their crimes had been to use their Yahoo email accounts to forward a secret Party directive on how to censor coverage of the Beijing Massacre during its anniversary. When pressured by the Party, Yahoo's China operation had revealed their names and addresses, leading to their arrests and imprisonment.

When the incident produced some scathing congressional criticism of Yahoo, in 2007 the company set up a $17 million assistance fund for human rights activists and designated Wu as its executor. A press release described the fund as designed "to provide humanitarian and legal aid to dissidents who have been imprisoned for expressing their views online." Yahoo CEO Jerry Yang described it as a demonstration that "our actions match our values."

However, it was not long before several of those who had been arrested filed a complaint in a U.S. federal court alleging that Yahoo had been careless in allowing Wu and his Laogai Research Foundation to have so much discretionary power over the fund that he could funnel more of its resources to his own projects than to those of others.

Then came a second wave of accusations against Wu, involving sexual harassment, domestic abuse, and bullying. The ambiguity these charges cast over Wu as a person and his human rights efforts was deeply unsettling. However, the recognition that this man was not an unalloyed hero was hardly a revelation for me. While working with him, I had seen signs of a totalism, and sometimes even a fanaticism, that he brought to almost everything he did.

Even more dispiriting for me than these allegations against Wu was the recognition that such tendencies were hardly his alone. During my years in and around China, I encountered all too many other such troubled and compromised Chinese human rights champions. It turned out that those who found enough backbone to stand up against the injustices of Mao's revolution were frequently so deeply scarred by the experience of abuse and imprisonment, sometimes in ways they did not even recognize themselves, that they had difficulty living balanced lives.

Should that be such a surprising revelation? After all, the whole point of the Party's oppression was to break the will of those who resisted its dictates and silence them. To accomplish those ends, the Party stopped at nothing, and the effects of this oppression on their victims was all too often profound.

I had met too many "dissidents" who appeared heroic from a distance, because they had bravely and resolutely stood up and resisted injustice. Who does not admire such a hero? However, when one got to know these "heroes" better, it all too often became evident that in the process of resisting oppression, they had suffered grievous psychological damage, if not physical harm. Even those lucky enough to end up in exile living in an open society often brought with them unhealable wounds that made it difficult for them to maintain healthy friendships, collegiate relationships, good work relations, or lasting marriages, much less a modicum of concord and happiness in their own lives.

The bitter reality was that the extremism of the Chinese Communist Revolution had emotionally damaged people in ways that rendered all too many of them hardly able to function in a healthy manner. The human consequences of China's tectonic revolution were both profound and subtle, but often of an invisible psychological nature that researchers and scholars have had an extremely difficulty time quantifying, much less understanding. So, precisely because the impacts of political repression were difficult to pin down, they often got left out of historical analyses of cause and effect.

Among my acquaintance with Chinese dissidents, one of the rare exceptions to this pattern was the prominent astrophysicist Fang Lizhi, whom my wife and I had gotten to know well while he was still in China in the 1980s. After being dismissed in 1987 from his job heading China's University of Science and Technology in Hefei, Fang was expelled from the Party and marginalized. Then, even though they had played no direct role in the preceding demonstrations, in the aftermath of the Beijing Massacre he and his wife felt so imperiled that they sought refuge in the U.S. Embassy in Beijing. There they lived hidden in complete sequestration for a year before the Chinese government finally allowed them to go into exile.

Once in Arizona, Fang and his physicist wife, Li Shuxian, managed to reboot their lives as academics and lead a relatively stable existence. But this was only possible because Fang was already an established senior scientist with a prestigious job in China. Such an established past helped stabilize him as he sought to rebuild a new life abroad.

However, even though Wu and I had worked well together, I often had intimations of just how injurious his agonizing years in prison camps had been to him as a younger man. He could be rigid, defiant, relentless, paranoid, and obsessive, all traits that were understandable given the duress he had been under for almost two decades. Alas, during his long imprisonment he had become someone who could never fully develop the kind of trust that enables a human being to live a reasonably complete and comfortable life. As Wu wrote later about why he joined our *60 Minutes* project, "I had to admit there was something darker about my mission. I needed to go back, needed to play with fire, needed to run with the bulls. . . . My whole life had been about testing the system, taunting the system, surviving the system, and now that I was a free man in the West, I could not stay away."

Wu's final denouement made it painfully obvious that when a human being is subjected to such extreme and relentless forms of repression, humiliation, and even torture, acts of resistance often cripple in ways that make a person more prone to aberrant behavior later in life. By his own admission, Wu had been compelled to do things just to survive that would have left any human being feeling fatally compromised, just as

Primo Levi had chronicled in his tormented work about his life in the German lagers.

Wu was neither the first, nor would he be the last, Chinese who—despite (or perhaps because of) their tenacious commitment to justice, liberty, freedom, and fairness in the face of repression—had suffered so grievously that their ability to function in a reasonably normal way in everyday society was undermined.

So, the news of Wu's death did fill me with a welter of conflicting feelings. While I had no way to judge his actual guilt or innocence, the denouement of his life was a lesson of sorts about the hidden psychological consequences of political oppression even for those survivors stalwart enough to resist against it. We ordinary mortals may find such heroic archetypes inspiring, but, as I had become painfully aware, there was too often a very steep personal price to be paid for such heroism, especially in China. Wu paid that price, several times over.

Chapter Twenty One

SOME HISTORICAL REFLECTIONS

A QUESTION that has always perplexed me was one that Gelber raised right after Ed Bradley's interview with Vice Minister Tong. He asked what I thought Chinese officials were thinking to themselves when they felt obliged to dissemble and lie in making public responses to politically sensitive questions?

Did they know they were being untruthful but not care?

Did they have private regret over not being able to respond more honestly?

Did they experience embarrassment, or were the imperatives of staying within the defined boundaries of the Party's current narrative so great that truthfulness as an operating principle had been so effectively disarmed they had no shame about lying? Or had they become so accustomed to almost autonomically obeying the Party's dicta that when required to be deceitful, they experienced no moral quandary?

Another question I had also always wondered about was related: Whence came Chinese officialdom's compulsion to present Potemkin village–like versions of almost everything, which was also a form of deceitfulness? Why was it so important for them always to have China appear perfect, even when it, and the rest of the world, was manifestly imperfect? Was it because, in their heart of hearts, officials knew from having lived inside Mao's revolution just how abysmally it had failed but, because of its loudly proclaimed national self-pretension to having achieved "greatness," they could not afford to acknowledge that failure publicly? Under such circumstances, there was only one face-saving option: Confect a Potemkin-like version of reality.

A "Potemkin village" has come to mean an ersatz place designed to falsely impress. It derives from a bit of Russian history that, although quasi-mythical, kept getting repeated because it perfectly highlighted the all-too-human urge to make things under one's aegis look better than they actually were. The meme originated in pre-Communist Russia under Tsarina Catherine the Great when, as the story goes, she appointed her former lover Prince Grigory Potemkin as the governor of Crimea, which Russia had recently annexed from the Ottoman Empire. When Potemkin learned that Catherine would visit the Crimea on an inspection tour, he was said to have been so eager to impress her that he ordered up a frieze of fake facades that he could prop up along the Dnieper River, to be accessorized with imported peasants waving cheerfully among flocks of fattened livestock and sacks of sand masquerading as stores of wheat. Potemkin's aspiration was to create the semblance of a prosperous modern village to impress Her Highness with his prowess as she floated downstream.

But the prince did not stop there! He was said to have cleverly designed his facades like stage sets so that they were transportable and could be reerected farther downstream to serially impress her highness with his gubernatorial prowess as she continued her riverine inspection tour.

The desire to show to one's advantage is, of course, hardly unique to Russian or Chinese leaders. Throughout world history, rulers have been vulnerable to excessive vanity, pride, and ambition, what the ancient Greeks knew as *hubris*. Then as now, when overreach ended in embarrassing failure, artifice was a way for a leader to save face.

The fixation on appearances that CCP leaders have so often evinced, especially when visiting foreign delegations appear, has always struck me as both Potemkin-like and absurd, especially after the 1980s, when China had at last started to generate so many real success stories that spoke for themselves without any deception.

Of course, the Chinese version of Prince Potemkin's insecurity complex grew out of China's own unique historical experience, one in which the impulse to deceive was fired by a national narrative of aggrievement, victimization, and "humiliation" (耻辱) that impelled so many of China's leaders to deploy dissimulation and deception on a mass scale. Simply put, they wanted to avoid revealing any hint of weakness or backwardness that might make them appear fallible and their country incompetent and still mired in its failed past. This dynamic became especially evident and extreme when it came to impressing visiting Americans, whom the Party viewed as not only innately prejudiced, but always eager to find evidence of failure in China's vaunted socialist revolution. It did not help that the Chinese themselves had a trope that "the foreign moon was rounder than the Chinese moon" (外国的月亮比中国的月亮圆).

Such a defensive compulsion was irrigated by China's history over the previous century and a half as the country suffered one indignity after another, being not only hectored, bullied, and colonialized, but looked down on for being incapable of defending even its territorial sovereignty against foreign incursion and occupation. What made this history an even greater humiliation for Chinese leaders was that, unlike counterparts in smaller countries with fewer pretentions, rulers of the "central kingdom" (中国) were traditionally accustomed to seeing themselves and their imperial system as the *ne plus ultra* of the civilized world: "all under heaven" (天下). In the view of educated Chinese, China was the earthly equivalent of the sun, sitting at the center of a heliocentric universe, around which all other lesser outlying lands obediently orbited like subsidiary planets.

The humiliation of being dispossessed through war and defeat at the hands of stronger imperial powers challenged China's historical sense of centrality and superiority. For both Communist and Nationalist leaders, this sense of dispossession generated an understandably powerful impulse to want cover up any and all other signs of weaknesses or backwardness lest further ignominy be heaped on them. And nowhere was there greater Chinese sensitivity than when under the censorious scrutiny of the so-called great powers.

To this day, whenever Chinese Communist officials find themselves embarrassingly exposed, their response mechanism has been almost autonomic: Reject the judgment, rail against whoever is doing the exposing, punish the offender, and cover up whatever was exposed as quickly as possible. This has led to a chronic tendency to attack both domestic and foreign critics with a totalism equivalent to an extreme allergic reaction.

Alas, since such knee-jerk responses have too often required a defense of the indefensible and no small amount of duplicity, instead of muting foreign criticisms, they too often only created more. At the same time, such defensive responses often made otherwise intelligent and articulate Chinese spokespeople appear disingenuous, even delusional.

Throughout the making of our *60 Minutes* program, I had been painfully aware that we were going to trigger another round of precisely this kind of destructive dynamic. Bradley's interview with Vice Minister Tong was a perfect example of how it worked: Tong needed to stay on script to mollify his superiors, who could take punitive action against him if he acknowledged any embarrassing wrongdoing. But because Bradley lived outside of China and could thus raise sensitive questions without fearing retaliation, he had no such fears. In fact, he relished the idea of bearding the Chinese dragon and Vice Minister Tong. Not only did he have veracity on his side, but such takedown confrontations were exactly what made *60 Minutes* such a popular investigative television program. So, even when presented with incontrovertible evidence on camera before the world, Tong was unable acknowledge that China continued to officially condone, even encourage, the use of political imprisonment and forced labor in the manufacture of goods for export. To do so would not only have overtly contradicted the Party's "correct line" (正确的路线) and violated his oath to maintain Party discipline, but been humiliating.

As Xi Jinping's father, Xi Zhongxun, tirelessly counseled his son, "The Party's interest comes first." And this Party penchant for distorting the truth went deep into a complex tangle of culture, history, politics, and psychology—a treacherous area of study for most scholars, writers, and policy specialists loath to open themselves up to accusations that they lack academic rigor by wandering into the bog of such speculation.

The Party's epic bouts of dissimulation also had roots in certain cultural traditions, such as the Chinese imperative to maintain "face" (面子), rather than "lose face" (丢脸). This is one more area of study that, because it is largely psychological rather than political or cultural, has remained a poorly understood aspect of Chinese life.

Suffice it to say, these sensitive nerves were only rendered more sensitive when the technologically advanced West arrived off the South China coast in the mid-nineteenth century with their powerful modern gunboats and defeated China in two Opium Wars. Being so humiliatingly vanquished sent the Qing Dynasty into a tailspin of self-doubt, decline, and lost face. These sensitivities only intensified with the dynasty's collapse in 1911 as China plunged into such a state of disunity and disarray that Sun Yat-sen derogatorily described it as "a dish of loose sand" (一盘散沙). And further humiliations were to come, starting with the embarrassing factoid that Sun lasted only three months as provisional president of China's first republic.

Despite the ignominies of China's modern history, the country's people never surrendered their pride, and the ensuing century was spent agonizing over how to expel foreign domination, "build a new country" 建国), bring about national "rejuvenation" (复兴), and regain respect (尊重). Then, in 1917, came Vladimir Lenin's *Imperialism: The Highest Stage of Capitalism*. It offered an explanation of how great powers imperialized, colonialized, exploited, subjugated, oppressed, victimized, and humiliated weaker countries like China to prolong their own capitalist systems and maintain their global domination. Lenin's treatise was a welcome tonic for smarting Chinese political leaders and intellectuals struggling to explain their country's backwardness and decline.

By dividing nations into two opposing blocs—the victimizing imperialists and the imperialized victims—Lenin gave China's new revolutionaries permission to view their country's dynastic collapse as thrust upon them by stronger, predatory, and avaricious imperialist powers. Among the consequences of his new vision of the world was a crystallization of strong anti-Western sentiment and a new nationalism that promised to help unify the Chinese people in opposition to the rapacious imperialist "great powers."

Lenin's narrative of a technologically advanced and militarily powerful colonialist West exploiting a technologically backward and weaker East found ready reception not only in China but also in other Asian colonies then under the dominion of France, Holland, Britain, Japan, Belgium, Portugal, Australia, and the United States. As the Soviet Union dispatched Comintern agents to China in the 1920s, this Leninist narrative was embraced not only by Sun Yat-sen and Chiang Kai-shek's Nationalist Party (KMT) but also by Li Dazhao, Chen Duxiu, and Mao Zedong's Communist Party (CCP). When Japan began its outright occupation of China in the 1930s, Chiang felt so assaulted and aggrieved he began daily entries in his journal with "Never Forget National Humiliation" (勿忘国耻) and even established a National Humiliation Day (国耻纪念日) to remind his people of their "century of humiliation" (百年国耻).

After the CCP's founding in 1921, this plaint became a key element in Mao's chiliastic vision of Marxism-Leninism leapfrogging from one country to another fomenting world revolution. It also became a convenient way to attribute China's parlous state of affairs to foreign oppression rather than its own developmental shortcomings. According to such logic, any self-acknowledged weakness would only contribute to a perception of revolutionary failure, exactly what China's twentieth-century CCP leaders most wanted to avoid.

One of the most pernicious results of all this sensitivity to any manifestation of weakness was that even during periods of the most savage self-inflicted chaos and violence under Mao, denials of the Party's responsibility became the norm. While Chinese society was being eviscerated by Mao's most destructive political campaigns—the Anti-Rightist Campaign, the Great Leap Forward, and the Great Proletarian Cultural Revolution—the appellation "great" was used as if even the most catastrophic self-induced failures could be rendered "great" simply by being called that.

Still standing now in Tiananmen Square is the Great Hall of the People (人民大会堂), and still hanging on Tiananmen Gate is the portrait of the Great Helmsman Mao Zedong (伟大的舵手毛泽东). Why? Because to take it down this iconic portrait would force the Party to acknowledge that Mao had been a disastrous mistake with virtually no redeeming graces. That, in turn, would precipitate a grievous loss of face for all those leaders throughout the decades who had proclaimed him as China's "great saving star" (伟大救星).

After all, a supreme revolutionary leader can never be "wrong" without triggering an avalanche of doubts about the very revolution of which they were the "grand progenitor" (太祖), as founders of each imperial dynasty were once known.

The great Belgian/Australian sinologist Pierre Ryckmanns, alias Simon Leys, described this kind of Communist legerdemain as a "jolly art that enables the Supreme Leader never to make mistakes—for even if he did the wrong thing, he did it at the right time, which makes it right for him to have been wrong, whereas the Enemy, even if he did the right thing, did it at the wrong time, which makes it wrong for him to have been right."

If there were ever wrongs that triggered criticism and face issues for China's Communist leadership, one was most surely its dedication to political imprisonment and forced labor. Not even Stalin bragged about his gulag. Although Communist parties have always relied on such brutal control mechanisms for dissidents, they have usually been abashed by them, especially when their retrograde nature was publicly exposed abroad. But since the Party was not about to give up its prison labor camps, leaders had no alternative but to try to keep them hidden from outside scrutiny. But, of course, sometimes they were embarrassingly exposed. It was precisely this vérité that made our *60 Minutes* venture so sensitive.

Chapter Twenty Two

THEN AND NOW

BY THE time I reconnected with my slumbering manuscript, Xi Jinping had been on his latter-day dragon throne for a decade, and his increasingly autocratic rule did not portend well for those still trapped in China's reform-through-labor prison system. Under his rule, this penal system not only gained new importance and more state funding, but had more fulsomely than ever entered global supply chains. Nowhere had this system grown more rapidly and become a more important regional economic driver than in Xinjiang, the province in which Wu had been arrested on his last trip to China.

In response to Beijing's repressive policies in Xinjiang Province during the mid-1990s, Islamist protesters became more vocal. After demonstrations against anti-Uyghur racism turned violent in 2009, the central government cracked down. But it was two bloody Muslim terrorist attacks in 2014 that triggered an even more severe wave of government repression against Uyghurs. The first attack took place in the city of Kunming, the capital of Yunnan Province, where thirty-one people were brutally killed during an Islamist assault on the city's train station. The second involved a series of assaults that spring against Han Chinese in Xinjiang itself, after which many Uyghurs were wounded, killed, or arrested during the ensuing "Special Operation to Severely Crack Down on Violent Terrorist Activities" (严厉打击暴力恐怖活动专项行动).

Human Rights Watch reported that during this campaign, up to a million Muslims and other Turkic people living in Xinjiang were arbitrarily detained and then incarcerated in more than three hundred newly built facilities, euphemistically called "vocational skills education training centers" (职业技能教培中心). The report claimed that many people had been detained simply for "attending religious events and ceremonies, studying religion, living in households with a 'dense religious atmosphere,' or wearing headscarves or beards."

The object of this crackdown was unsentimentally described in a 2017 New China News Agency Weibo posting by Maisumujiang Maimuer, a religious affairs official in the province, as designed not only to "break their [Uyghur] lineage, break their roots, break their connections, and break their origins," but to "completely shovel up the roots . . . of these two-faced people."

As the campaign progressed, the UN Committee on the Elimination of Racial Discrimination accused Beijing of turning Xinjiang "into something that resembled a massive internment camp shrouded in secrecy, a sort of no-rights zone." Other investigations charged the Chinese government with compelling Uyghur detainees not only to live and work in local prison camp factories but sometimes to be transferred to factories thousands of miles away.

"It is extremely difficult for Uyghurs to refuse or escape these work assignments, which are enmeshed with the apparatus of detention and political indoctrination both inside and outside Xinjiang," noted a report from the Australian Strategic Policy Institute. "In addition to constant surveillance, the threat of arbitrary detention hangs over minority citizens who refuse their government-sponsored work assignments."

As it turned out, some of the plants to which detainees were being sent fed into the supply chains of well-known global brands such as Apple, BMW, Gap, Huawei, Nike, Samsung, Sony, and Volkswagen, a revelation that only helped internationalize the impact of these abuses.

In December 2021, Geoffrey Nice, a British lawyer who had headed the UN war crimes tribunal prosecuting former Serbian President Slobodan Milošević, charged the Chinese government with committing possible genocide in Xinjiang. His report not only provided a summary of evidence but also spelled out the international law that obliged other countries to act as soon as they learned that crimes such as torture, sexual violence, the destruction of religious and cultural practices, the disappearance of people, forced birth control, the separation of children from families, and forced labor in commercial enterprises were taking place.

The PRC embassy in London dismissed Nice's report as nothing more than a "pseudo tribunal" and a "political tool used by a few anti-China and separatist elements to deceive and mislead the public."

As the Beijing Winter Olympic Games were approaching in 2022, the number of international investigations into rights abuses in Xinjiang proliferated. On December 23, 2021, U.S. President Joe Biden signed the Uyghur Forced Labor Prevention Act, legislation designed to shield American consumers from China's newly fledged forced labor practices by requiring U.S. companies importing from Xinjiang Province to prove that the goods they were importing were not made "in whole or part" by forced labor.

Clothing, footwear, automobile parts, poultry, tomato products, home appliances, solar panels, and electronics were all categories in which Xinjiang producers excelled. For example, one of every five cotton garments sold globally was estimated to contain some Xinjiang-grown cotton. By then the province was producing some 90 percent of China's cotton and 20 percent of the world's supply. Since Xinjiang-sourced cotton was often mixed together with stock grown elsewhere, foreign importers of garments and other finished goods containing Xinjiang cotton found themselves confronted by inspection requirements that were costly and extremely difficult to meet.

Even the World Bank found itself accused of abuses, just as Wu had suspected when he went to Xinjiang to investigate this issue back in the mid-1990s. The Atlantic Council, a Washington-based think tank, obtained "significant evidence" showing that global institutions such as the International Finance Corporation (IFC), a member of the World Bank Group, had provided hundreds of millions of dollars in loans to prison-related enterprises in Xinjiang that very likely relied on forced Uyghur labor. This report further alleged that the

IFC was only one of the bank's "active participants" to have signed off on some $486 million in direct loans and equity investments for Xinjiang-based enterprises, some of which were using forced labor made up of Uyghur workers who had been removed from their native land in an effort to dilute Muslim cultural practices in the province.

"The World Bank exists to support global development, not to finance modern slavery," chided Samuel Cogolati, a Belgian parliamentarian, who had himself been sanctioned by the Chinese government for sponsoring an EU debate resolution on the issue. "There can be no further excuses," he continued. Complicit corporations "must divest from these companies linked to forced labor abuses immediately."

One might have thought that this avalanche of critical investigative news articles, think tank reports, and government studies would have goaded Chinese leaders into confronting at least some of their alleged abuses. However, instead of moderating the policies, Xi Jinping continued to urge officials in Xinjiang, as he had in 2014, to show "absolutely no mercy" in what he characterized as a life-and-death "struggle against terrorism, infiltration and separatism."

In May 2022, former Chilean President Michelle Bachelet, who had become High Commissioner for Human Rights at the UN Human Rights Council, alleged there was sufficient evidence to charge that "serious human rights violations" were being perpetrated against Uyghur Muslims in Xinjiang. However, when it came time to vote on whether to debate the issue, because of pressure from Beijing and client countries, for only the second time in the council's history the motion failed.

The UN Human Rights Council's concern for what was going on in Xinjiang saw an even more ignominious chapter unfold when Bachelet herself made an ill-fated "investigative" trip to the province. During her six-day visit, she was afforded no opportunities to meet with representatives from independent organizations, listen to any unmonitored nongovernmental voices, or make any independent inquiries on her own into what was actually happening among Xinjiang's Uyghur community. When she failed to be more demanding of her hosts about her very limited schedule, the global press pilloried her as being too accommodating to the Chinese government.

Insult was added to injury when Xi Jinping himself used a videoed meeting with Bachelet in Beijing as an opportunity to publicly excoriate her and the UN for deigning to concern themselves with human rights abuses in China. "There is no perfect 'ideal country' on the human rights issue, and there is no need for a 'teacher' who commands other countries," Xi sanctimoniously lectured her. "We can't politicize and instrumentalize the human rights issue, engage in double standards, and use human rights as an excuse to interfere in the internal affairs of other countries." Xi went on to decry Western criticisms as "deviating from reality" and to reject the notion that liberal democracies provided a model for China to follow. "Completely copying the institutional model of other countries," he chided, would only "bring disastrous consequences" to China.

The U.S. State Department spokesman under President Biden, Ned Price, described Bachelet's visit as "a mistake," saying it was unacceptable for her to have "agreed to a visit under these circumstances, where the High Commissioner will not be granted the type of unhindered access, free and full access, that would be required to do a complete assessment, and to come back with a full picture of the atrocities, the crimes against humanity, and the genocide ongoing in Xinjiang."

"The dynamics surrounding the U.N. human rights commissioner's visit were part of the larger pattern in which Beijing, through manipulation and intimidation, seeks to shape behaviors and norms in line with authoritarian preferences," wrote *Washington Post* columnist Josh Rogin. "Leaders in Beijing are now surely more confident than ever they can commit mass atrocities without fearing significant costs imposed by the international community. When the history books are written about the world's failure to stop the Uyghur genocide, Bachelet's trip will go down as one of many shameful episodes."

Bachelet's Potemkin-ized tour of Xinjiang was a sad reminder that, far from being tempered by three decades of engagement, China's systems of arbitrary detention, imprisonment, and forced labor had instead been modernized and expanded. By the end of 2024, the Uyghurs Human Rights Project was reporting that statistics released by the Xinjiang Autonomous Uyghurs Region itself showed that one in twenty-six Uyghurs in the region had been imprisoned, making this the highest rate of ethnic imprisonment in the world.

"Uyghur and other non-Han people in the Uyghur region were estimated to be imprisoned at just over 47 times the rate of Han people," claimed the report. Many of those detained were forced to work in detention center factories. The situation in Xinjiang had become grave enough that James Millward, a

Georgetown University scholar whose specialty was Uyghur studies, called Beijing's policies an "attempt to find a final solution to the Xinjiang problem."

If there was a single personification of the increasingly repressive nature of Beijing's approach toward Xinjiang's Muslims, it was the case of the well-known Uyghur anthropologist Rahile Dawut. Her academic field of study was customs at local mosques, or *mazars*, many of which were now being either closed or turned into tourist sites.

In 2017, while on a trip to Beijing, where she had received her graduate training, Dawut vanished. For months there was no official explanation of her disappearance. It was not until 2018 that the American human rights monitoring group, the Dui Hua Foundation, learned she had been arrested for "endangering national security" and sentenced at a secret court hearing to life imprisonment for "splittism" and the advocacy of "political separatism."

Adding more tinder to the Xinjiang fire, when demonstrations broke out against Xi's zero COVID policy in the winter of 2022, one of the events that sent people spilling out of their government-enforced home sequestration into the streets of Shanghai holding up sheets of blank white paper as a form of protest, were social media posts reporting that ten Uyghurs had just been burned to death in an Urumqi high-rise apartment because authorities had locked the building's fire exits as part of Xi's strict COVID regimen.

Even though Xi rejected foreign criticism of Xinjiang as a form of meddling in China's internal affairs, a growing number of foreign companies working there were forced to begin recognizing that they had a problem. Although finding alternative sourcing options in other countries was difficult, nonetheless many started inching toward a China exit. However, because they feared punitive retaliation against their other corporate interests in China, most CEOs did so as unobtrusively as possible.

One country that found itself caught in the middle was Germany. Over the past decades, it had made many large and profitable investments in China. But now, as Xi's crackdown against the Uyghurs advanced, it found itself forced to reckon with the consequences of having allowed several of its key industrial sectors to become overly dependent on one key market.

As late as 2024, the world's largest industrial chemicals company, Germany's BASF, was still trying to expand in China by building a $11.5 billion petrochemical and power-generating plant in Guangdong. At the same time, its executives were beginning to recognize that there were brand damage dangers to staying in China. One of BASF's wake-up calls came when a key ingredient used to make Spandex in one of its China plants was reported by a human rights group to be made with forced labor. Despite its fears of retaliation, BASF finally acknowledged human rights violations that it found "incompatible" with its values and began seeking to sell interests in its two Xinjiang plants. It was hardly a surprise when the company ran into difficulty getting Chinese government permission to do so.

Volkswagen, another iconic German corporation, also had some joint venture manufacturing facilities in Xinjiang. Since the company had for decades derived substantial revenue from making and selling German cars in China, its executives were apprehensive about even hinting that they might be considering closing their Xinjiang auto plant and withdrawing from the province. As Patricia Nilsson bluntly explained in the *Financial Times*, a VW pullout from Xinjiang "would anger its local partners which were owned by the Chinese state."

But when some of Volkswagen's exported vehicles were held up at American ports over "a customs issue," after it was revealed that their engines used electronic components made with forced labor in Xinjiang, the company was forced to confront the issue. This led to "advanced talks" with VW's Chinese partner, the giant state-owned Shanghai Automotive Industry Corporation (SAIC), about spinning off VW's interests in their 2013 joint venture.

Few were surprised when China's Ministry of Foreign Affairs denounced VW's concerns about forced labor in Xinjiang as "a lie of the century concocted by anti-China forces to discredit China." The ministry went on to warn, "We hope the enterprises concerned will respect the facts, recognize right and wrong and cherish the opportunity to invest and develop in Xinjiang."

In November 2024, Volkswagen was finally able to transfer ownership of its two Xinjiang production facilities and its test track to the Chinese, although the cost was high and the brand damage real.

Such conflicts caused the *New York Times* to observe that China was becoming an increasingly difficult place to do business. "China does not allow independent supply chain audits in Xinjiang," it said. It "even detained employees of foreign due diligence companies who work in far less politically sensitive places like Beijing and Shanghai."

Soon other foreign companies that had become increasingly dependent on Chinese markets also ended up in the forced labor cross fire. Calvin Klein and Tommy Hilfiger, both owned by parent company PVH, found themselves in a bind as they tried to comply with the Uyghur Forced Labor Prevention Act by disentangling their supply chains from cotton produced in Xinjiang. But as they discreetly sought a remedy, China's Ministry of Commerce charged them with taking actions that "seriously damages the legitimate rights and interests of relevant Chinese companies and endangers China's sovereignty, security and development interests." Then, PVH was put on China's "entities list," the first time Beijing had blacklisted a U.S. company with such large business interests in China.

And when, in order to meet foreign customs requirements, executives at the international clothing manufacturer Uniqlo insisted that their company use no contraband cotton from Uyghur ethnic regions, social media inside China erupted in protest over their statement. Under the hashtag "I support Xinjiang cotton" a campaign called for a boycott against Uniqlo just for seeking to clean its supply chain of contraband cotton.

As Michael Hart, president of the American Chamber of Commerce, glibly observed, all these measures and countermeasures "certainly put a chill on the business environment."

As more and more foreign companies became ensnarled in supply chain problems, the Xinjiang drama sometimes reached almost comical extremes. For example, in 2024 Francesco

Mutti, the fourth generationfamily leader of Mutti Tomatoes in Parma, Italy, became embroiled in the fray. With some 23 percent of the world's tomato production now being sourced from Xinjiang, an outraged Mutti called on the EU to approve new tariffs against China to stop what he called "environmental dumping" in Italy.

"The objective," he exploded, "is to give tomatoes their dignity, to take a product that has often been considered just a commodity and say, 'No—tomatoes count!'"

There were elements of both comedy and tragedy in the growing challenges China's supply chains posed to the system of world trade. While nobody seemed to have an answer about how to make China respond more constructively to the democratic world's concerns over human rights issues like forced labor, at least officials in the Biden administration were still willing to talk about them.

Chapter Twenty Three

THE PAST AS PROLOGUE

IN THE 1990S, despite their two very different political systems, the United States and China continued to seek ways to coexist and avoid conflict. Things were not perfect, but despite all the points of divergence—ideology, political imprisonment, dumping, IP theft, Taiwan, etc.—it was still possible to imagine that increased interaction might lead to greater convergence. Even in the wake of the 1989 Beijing Massacre, when all seemed lost, Deng Xiaoping and then Communist Party General Secretary Jiang Zemin succeeded in managing the U.S.-China relationship in ways that enabled both sides to remain hopeful that certain aspects of "reform and opening" might continue to haltingly help improve rather than erode U.S.-China relations. As late as 2009, such efforts enabled President Barack Obama to hope, "The rise of a strong, prosperous China can be a source of strength for the community of nations."

However, as China fell under the sway of Xi Jinping's leadership in 2012, his devotion to a Leninist political model for China and to an increasingly hostile Cold War–like vision of U.S.-China relations rendered Obama's hope more and more a pipe dream. It became increasingly clear, at least to me, that a society that had undergone a revolutionary upheaval as deep, long, and violent as China's could not expect to easily escape the enduring influences of that experience. Even when a visionary pragmatist like Deng Xiaoping mounted the political stage, waved his figurative wand of reform, and proclaimed a bold new societal direction, the gravity of Mao's revolutionary past remained inescapable. China under Xi, like Russia under Putin, was a living demonstration of how difficult it can be for countries and their societies to escape their pasts. "What's past is prologue," Shakespeare famously proclaimed. China's past and its deeply rooted system of authoritarian rule seemed unlikely to be eclipsed anytime soon.

Westerners were drawn to the promise that "peaceful evolution" (和平演变) offered the prospect of a slow and nonviolent transition from the past to a different and less tumultuous present and future for China. However, Xi Jinping did not share that fantasy. For him, "peaceful evolution" implied not a gradual and pacific passage to a more stable and open future, but the dismantling of China's one-party state and the end of the CCP's unilateral rule. This scenario was exactly what Xi viewed as having led to the catastrophic downfall of the Soviet Union in 1989, and he was not about to preside over a similar self-immolation of his own centralized autocratic control. As good Leninists in China were coming to recognize, Deng

Xiaoping's policies of "reform and opening," if left unchecked, would lead not just to a form of "peaceful evolution" but to the demise of the CCP and the PRC, just as *glasnost* and *perestroika* had ineluctably led to the demise of the CPSU and the USSR.

As a result, Xi eschewed reform and instead moved to strengthen the CCP. An important piece of his Party-strengthening agenda was not only keeping its penal institutions and reform-through-labor system functional, but strengthening them with the latest technologies. Never again would the Party allow the kind of social latitude Wu had exploited as he roamed unmonitored around the countryside exposing the darkest side of what Xi had come to call "the China story" (中国故事). Nowhere in China was the reimposition of Party mechanisms and updated forms of imprisonment more in evidence than in Xinjiang, where Wu was arrested on his last ill-fated trip to his homeland.

After three decades of hoping, perhaps naively, that China might somehow permanently temper its revolutionary past, I reread my manuscript. China was still confronting the questions of political imprisonment and forced labor. And once again these questions had started bedeviling China's relations with democratic countries.

However, making matters more complicated was the reality that during the glory days of "engagement" and the reckless adoption of "globalization" as a win-win strategy, these very democracies had become so dependent on supply chains "coupling" them to China that "decoupling" (脱钩) because of prison labor or other thorny political issues was no easy matter. Making the situation even more intractable was the reality that some of the natural resources and manufactured goods that China controlled, and that other countries needed most, were now enmeshed with prison and forced labor issues, especially in Xinjiang. Polysilicon, photovoltaic cells, solar panels, batteries, electric vehicles, wind generators, and critical minerals were all commodities that China had a lock on but the rest of the world urgently needed.

Xinjiang's sandy deserts provided up to 45 percent of the world's solar grade silicon, and more than 92 percent of solar cell manufacturing was being done in China. Seven of the world's top ten solar panel producers were now based in Xinjiang, giving China a choke hold over this critical global supply chain. And China had acquired other choke holds over critical renewable energy sources, technologies, rare earths, and critical minerals on which Beijing leaders had a near monopoly. This created choke points that both sides began using as political levers in what was becoming an increasingly punitive struggle as the world's global trade systems and radically differing political ideologies collided.

In the increasingly fraught world of U.S.-China bilateral trade, Thea Lee, deputy undersecretary for international affairs at the U.S. Labor Department, warned in May 2024 that Uyghur laborers were now being forcibly transferred from Xinjiang to factories elsewhere in China. This was a move designed by Beijing to thwart U.S. corporate efforts to verify that supply chains that reached into Xinjiang were free of prison labor.

In June 2025, the *New York Times*, the German newsmagazine *Der Spiegel*, and the Bureau of Investigative Journalism ran a joint story entitled "Far from Home: Uyghur Workers in Factories Supplying Global Brands." It revealed how tens of thousands of Uyghur workers had been strong-armed into accepting transfers from Xinjiang to factories elsewhere in China as a way to mask the use of forced labor. With the problem no longer largely limited geographically to Xinjiang, it became infinitely more difficult for foreign companies to monitor and control.

"Human rights advocates were reporting that Uyghurs have little choice but to accept such assignments outside Xinjiang," wrote *Der Spiegel*. "If they refuse, they risked being labelled troublemakers, a serious charge in a region where people have been subjected to lengthy detentions for even the faintest signs of dissent or religious expression, like owning a Quran."

In our own *60 Minutes* investigation, we had discovered how tanned yak hides sourced in Qinghai Province were first sent to Hong Kong before being transshipped to Korea and turned into finished goods there, entitling them to be marketed in the United States with "Made in Korea" labels. Now the Chinese government was engaging in a new kind of subterfuge to thwart foreign efforts to block such goods from entering their countries.

In 2024, the European Union passed legislation designed to block goods made with forced labor in China from entering EU markets. However, in recognition of how difficult it would be for businesses to comply with the law, it delayed implementation until 2027. Even if some new sophisticated forms of detection were developed by then, Chinese officials would most certainly push back with the kinds of denials and disavowals offered up by Vice Minister Tong when he was grilled by Ed Bradley.

"We hope that certain people in the US administration will respect Xinjiang's achievements in stability and development, heed the call of Xinjiang's 25 million people of all ethnic groups, respect facts, and act responsibly, instead of being misled by fake news produced by certain media," Ministry of Foreign Affairs spokesman Wang Wenbin chided foreign critics as early as 2021, when he launched a webinar entitled "Xinjiang Is a Wonderful Land," cosponsored by China's Permanent Mission to the United Nations Office at Geneva and the government of Xinjiang Uyghur Autonomous Region. "We welcome fair-minded foreigners to visit Xinjiang and learn the real situation there," he continued. "At the same time, we are firmly opposed to interference in China's internal affairs by any country or individual under the pretext of human rights, and to the hyping-up of the so-called 'investigation' in Xinjiang by someone who is already convinced that we are guilty."

By September 2025, the Chinese government was even more militant in rebutting Western claims that forced labor and even some forms of genocide were being committed in Xinjiang. A statement entitled "The Successful Practice of the Party's Xinjiang Governance Strategy in the New Era" (新时代党的治疆方略的成功实践), issued by the State Council's Information Office (中华人民共和国国务院新闻办公室) and published by the *People's Daily* on September 21, laid out their argument:

> In recent years, a number of Western countries, led by the United States, have imposed sanctions on businesses and

individuals related to Xinjiang on the account of "genocide" and "forced labor"—lies and absurd fallacies they have concocted to interfere in China's internal affairs. Their purpose is political manipulation and economic bullying under the guise of human rights protection. Countering sanctions and interference is essential for breaking the containment of China by the anti-China forces in the US and some Western countries, which use Xinjiang as a handle. It is a just response for safeguarding our national sovereignty, security, and development interests.

Chapter Twenty Four

AND NOW FOR SOMETHING OLD

BY 2026 so much had changed since our *60 Minutes* program aired, one might have expected that China's Leninist system, too, would have undergone a metamorphosis. But the assumption, or hope, that China's "democratic dictatorship of the proletariat" would somehow be politically transformed by the Party's own regimen of "reform and opening" had turned out to be overly optimistic. So, starry-eyed liberal Westerners may be forgiven for feeling disappointed. After all, we were inclined to believe that history had a felicitous direction. Had not Martin Luther King oracularly proclaimed: "The arc of the moral universe is long, but it bends toward justice?"

Such hopes grew out of the work of people like the nineteenth-century German philosopher Georg Wilhelm Friedrich Hegel, who believed that history had a teleology, an understandable direction. In his view, history would inevitably bring about a gradual realization of greater freedom as the

World Spirit (*Weltgeist)* did its dialectical dance through time. Karl Marx not only borrowed Hegel's assumptions, but went him one better. He proclaimed that history's dialectical march forward was a form of "historical determinism" that would ultimately, and inevitably, bring about Communism. Americans, well-known for both their optimism and naivete, borrowed elements of both of these rather Pollyannaish views of history to allow themselves to imagine that history's development through time was a form of ineluctable progress. President Bill Clinton liked to proclaim that the United States was on "the right side of history," as if he, on behalf of America, had divined its direction. It was a nice dream—but only for those not accustomed to nightmares.

What distinguished Wu was his incapacity to buy into such visions of history as possessing an enlightened, progressive direction. The brutal way he had been treated during the Chinese Communist Revolution made it impossible for him to believe any such rose-tinted scenario lay at the heart of history's development. After all that he had suffered, for him it was hardly credible that the arc of history "bent" anywhere, much less in a promising direction.

"In my view the United States is still hoping that China's hybrid form of capitalism will turn to democracy," Wu caustically wrote after our program aired. "More likely it will lead to the creation of a new form of totalitarian, a super-nationalistic military state."

Wu penned those words during the heyday of engagement, when, despite all the impediments, many still dared hope that the PRC might make a piecemeal transition to some more open form of statecraft. Looking back on Wu's forecast now, it is impossible not to acknowledge its prescience. He foresaw almost exactly what did come to pass in his homeland, that the Party would finally pulled away from Deng's reformist agenda, as if drawn instinctually backward by some powerful magnetic force deep inside its political/cultural being that had always made it instinctually wary of losing control. And with Xi's retreat from reform went America's vaunted policy of "engagement" that had allowed China and the United States to muddle along in a relationship in which friendship and antagonism remained mixed, but still allowed for a functional interaction.

So, was "engagement" misguided from the outset?

No, it was not.

As a global leader, the United States was correct to do what it could to encourage China to effect a peaceful transition from the kind of violent revolutionary class struggle, mass movements, widespread political incarceration, endless social chaos, famine, and physical hardship that had characterized Mao's revolution to a more stable equilibrium that was less politically repressive at home and less antagonistic toward the outside world. Deng Xiaoping's reforms catalyzed such a course correction and, by doing so, allowed many during the 1980s to hope that changes might continue and become deeper and more enduring. It was paradoxically the mass demonstrations in 1989 demanding even more openness and democracy, the Beijing Massacre, and the ensuing political crackdown that ended this interlude of hope for a peaceful transition.

And yet after 1989 under Party General Secretary Jiang Zemin during the mid-1990s and early 2000s, there was a surprising recrudescence of reformist sentiment, especially on the economic side of the ledger. It was not until Hu Jintao assumed the leadership of the Party in 2002 that the promise of reform and engagement began to fade.

One of Hu's new and most disruptive conceits grew out of the conviction that China had certain nonnegotiable "core interests" (核心利益) and, now that it was wealthier and more powerful, it was honor bound to defend them, even by military force. These core interests had traditionally involved sovereign claims over Tibet, Xinjiang, Hong Kong, Macau, the Senkaku Islands, several disputed territories in India, and, of course, Taiwan. But Hu provocatively expanded the scope of China's "core interests" to include the South China Sea, all the way from Hainan Island down to the Natuna Islands off Indonesia. Everything within China's so-called nine-dash line that hung down off the South China Coast like a giant udder—including all the "landforms" and islands not explicitly within the twelve-mile territorial waters of neighboring states—was claimed as Chinese.

In the middle of this shift of thinking about China's place in the Asia Pacific, the 2009 financial crisis hit. From the perspective of Hu and many of his fellow Party leaders, this came as a sign that the United States was in decline, while China was rising. So, when Xi Jinping came to power in 2012, it was hardly surprising that he not only embraced these same presumptions about China's new core interests, but also began to centralize his own political authority at home and became far much more assertive on the global stage.

By the mid-2020s, China had gained so much new global clout that its leadership no longer felt obliged to show the kind of deference it once had to the great powers of old, especially the United States. Why, after finally attaining their century-long dream of "wealth and power" (富强), should China continue to accommodate the United States, a country that Xi was accustomed to describing as a "hostile foreign force" (境外敌对势力)? The concession making of the past had been the last resort of weak leaders like those who led China during its "hundred years of humiliation" (百年国耻). Now that things had changed, Xi no longer felt the need to be so deferential. Concessions and compromises that had once been viewed as necessary diplomatic tools to resolve complex disputes came to be seen as embarrassing hallmarks of weakness. And, if there was one thing that Xi and other ranking leaders wanted to avoid, it was any hints of weakness that might mar their carefully cultivated image of invincibility.

"China certainly in the past has not and, in the future, will not, accept the unwarranted accusations from the U.S. side," State Councilor and future Foreign Minister Wang Yi erupted at the 2021 meeting in Alaska attended by Secretary of State Anthony Blinken, National Security Advisor Jake Sullivan, and NSC Indo-Pacific Coordinator Kurt Campbell. "In the past several years, China's legitimate rights and interests have come under outright suppression, plunging the China-U.S. relationship into a period of unprecedented difficulty. This has damaged the interests of our two peoples and taken its toll on world stability and development, and this situation must no longer continue. China urges the U.S. side to fully abandon the hegemonic practice of willfully interfering in China's internal affairs. This has been a longstanding issue, and it should be changed. It is time for it to change."

If Western "hegemony" was waning and Chinese power waxing, why should Wang or Xi endure insulting criticisms about China being a retrograde, one-party tyranny dependent on penal colonies filled with political prisoners compelled to do force labor? After all that it had accomplished in terms of economic development, health care, education, transportation, and military modernization, had China not earned the right, even with its retrograde Leninist political system, to be accorded some "mutual respect and understanding" (相互尊重和理解), especially from the arrogant, and now increasingly dysfunctional and declining, democracies?

What Party leaders seemed to miss was a simple but elusive truth: Earning respect depends on acting respectably, certainly not maintaining, much less defending, an extensive gulag filled with political prisoners.

Whether or not China was deserving of respect—and in Xi's view it was—as he said as early as 2017, it was "time for us to take centre stage in the world and to make a greater contribution to humankind."

It was also time to become more assertive. If respect was not forthcoming, then Beijing would compel some submission, even muscle aside the United States and take the lead in setting up a new global order more congruent with Chinese Leninism than the West's arrogant but balky democratic conceits.

As the official *New China News Agency* put it, "China opposes all forms of hegemonism and power politics and rejects interference in other countries' internal affairs. The United States must conduct serious soul-searching. It must critically examine what it has done, let go of its arrogance and prejudice, and quit its hegemonic, domineering and bullying practices." And if China had to do a little "bullying" itself to demonstrate that it was no longer to be trifled with, was that not the prerogative of every great power? If the United States would not respect China, it might at least be brought to fear it.

Mao had defiantly declared, "The East wind is prevailing over the West wind" (东风压倒西风). Now Xi began echoing Mao with similar political homilies, "The East is rising and the West is declining" (东升西降), he proclaimed. And, he embellished, "Time and momentum are on our side" (时与势在我们一边).

With Xi becoming more authoritarian and flexing his global muscle around the world, many Americans began wondering: What's the point of continuing to cooperate, even trade, with China? Would not further collaboration and trade only assist it in becoming a better competitor and possibly even a more threatening adversary? It was this fundamental change in attitude that sounded the death knell for engagement.

As Xi's new assertiveness became ever more obvious, in a widely read 2018 article in *Foreign Affairs*, Kurt Campbell and Ely Ratner—the former in the U.S. Department of State, the latter in the U.S. Department of Defense—sounded the tocsin against China's new global pretensions. "Neither carrots nor sticks have swayed China as predicted," they wrote. "Diplomatic and commercial engagement have not brought political and economic openness. Growth was supposed to bring not just economic opening, but political liberalization. Neither US military power nor regional balancing has stopped Beijing from seeking to displace core components of the US-led system. And the liberal international order has failed to lure or bind China as powerfully as expected. China has instead pursued its own course, belying a range of American expectations in the process. . . . The record is increasingly clear that Washington once again put too much faith in its power to shape China's trajectory."

By 2023, things had become so strained during the Biden administration that when U.S. Secretary of Commerce Gina Raimondo returned from China to address a California business group, she described Xi's regime as "the biggest threat we've ever had. China is not our friend." And Director of National Intelligence Avril Haines, ended a congressional testimony by warning: "The CCP represents both the leading and most consequential threat to U.S. national security and leadership globally."

By that spring, 83 percent of Americans held either a "negative" or an "unfavorable" view of China, with almost 40 percent perceiving it as an outright "enemy," and only 6 percent viewing it as a "partner."

It was in the middle of this geopolitical inflexion point that I stumbled upon my old manuscript. As I reacquainted myself with what I had written, I was reminded that even though the world and China had changed radically since 1991, the political system that the People's Republic of China had borrowed from Stalin's USSR had not. Indeed, under Xi, its old political structure had only become more deeply confirmed. It was almost as if, reluctant to let go of its parlous past, China was now caught up in a new crypto-dynastic cycle.

During the nineteenth century, Western Christian missionaries and historians viewed the way each new imperial dynasty followed its precursor in cyclical fashion as suggesting a "changeless" circular aspect to Chinese history. They saw these cycles as driven by an innately conservative cultural impulse that favored historical continuity over linear progress. The highest aspiration of each new imperial lineage was to replace its failed predecessor with a more perfect replica of the Golden Age of Zhou, an idealized period of ancient history (1046 to 779 BCE) said to have been ruled over by a succession of "sage kings" (圣王) that Confucius had venerated as political exemplars.

■ ■ ■

The idea of dynastic cycles and a changeless China received three monumental drubbings in the twentieth century. The first came with the fall of its last dynasty, the Qing (清), in 1912, ending more than two millennia of its more or less continuous imperial system. The second came with the victory of Mao's Marxist-Leninist revolution in 1949 that quickly spawned endless mass political movements and campaigns designed to "overturn" (翻身) China's traditional "feudal order" and "liberate" its people to a utopian Marxist future. The third arrived with Deng Xiaoping's reform movement in the late 1970s and 1980s that brought a dramatic cancellation of major parts of Mao's revolution, enlivened China's economy with market forces, and invigorated its politics with an interlude of unprecedented openness.

Then came Xi Jinping and his efforts to fortify China and its Leninist past, even while forging forward economically, technologically, and militarily to play an ever more prominent global role. Far from receding into oblivion, China's old Stalinist system, complete with its vast penal colony, not only continued to be a structural part of China's modern economy but was being updated with modern technology. Like the metal nitinol that bends when heated only to snap back to its original shape upon being cooled—a phenomenon known in metallurgy as "shape memory"—despite all the efforts expended on bending and shaping through internal reform, revolution, external pressure, and foreign influence, China was evincing a tenacious tendency to return to something like its original form.

Part of Xi's playbook was a grand plan for a national "rejuvenation" (复兴) that would restore China to the level of global greatness he viewed it as formerly possessing. His aspiration was not unlike the traditional notion of "dynastic revival" (中兴) once embraced by emperors when they needed to stabilize and reinvigorate their own dynastic rule after times of stress and decline.

But as Xi began his third five-year term in office, what was striking about his notion of rejuvenation was its titanic ambition. Its grandness in scale suggested he was being driven as much by his own personal sense of deficiency as by an assessment of China's economic or national interests. This was hardly surprising, because Xi had been shaped, like all humans, during his formative teenage years. And for him, those years were a time of extreme upheaval, hardship, deprival, and an almost total absence of supportive parental presence.

In a 2025 biography of Xi's father, *The Party Comes First: The Life of Xi Zhongxun, Father of Xi Jinping*, Joseph Torigian offers some insights into the young Xi's formative experiences during a time of political tumult, treachery, violence, and betrayal. His father was a revolutionary colleague of Mao Zedong's who rose from a lowly peasant family into the Party elite to become a vice premier. However, in 1962 during one of Mao's endless political campaigns, Xi Zhongxun was labeled an "historical counterrevolutionary" (历史反革命分子), one of the most reviled categories of political damnation in the Maoist lexicon. His purge was a devastating experience for both father and son. With Xi Zhongxun cast out of the land of the living for sixteen years, his teenage son not only was denied a father during his most formative years but had to suffer the humiliation of a parent who had been relegated to the worst of the "five black categories" (黑五类).

When the Cultural Revolution erupted four years later, thirteen-year-old Xi Jinping was himself "sent down" (下放) to a penurious peasant village in Shaanxi, the province where his father had once presided as a regional leader. There he spent seven years as "an educated youth" (知识青年), forced to make his lonely way in a place where everyone knew of his famous father's ignominy. So great was that stigma that when Xi Jinping sought to join the Little Red Pioneers (红小队), a youth group entitling its young members to wear a prestigious red scarf, his application was rebuffed seven times because of his bad "family background" (家庭背景). Only on his eighth humiliating try was Xi finally accepted, and then only because one committee member was a family friend.

From such bitter Cultural Revolution experiences the young Xi learned that social and political acceptance required strict discipline and becoming "redder" and more politically orthodox and "correct" than others. He also learned that survival depended on remaining alert, to the point of paranoia, against political threats.

Chapter Twenty Five

A HIGHER STAGE OF COMMUNISM?

BY THE middle of 2026, with the war in Ukraine in its fourth year, an expansion of war in the Middle East with a US and Israeli attack on Iran, and the "family of nations" dividing into new blocs that look ever more like a Cold War 2.0—China, the DPRK, Iran, Belarus, and Russia in one camp, the democracies in the other—the world waited for the next shoe to drop, perhaps this time in the Taiwan Straits, the South China Sea, or the Senkaku Islands. If the new Cold War became a global hot war, this time the standoff would be not just between two clashing ideological systems but between two well-armed economic superpowers ruled by antithetical political systems and equally mercurial leaders. By 2025, Xi had rejiggered the term limits set by Deng Xiaoping to enable himself to remain in power like Stalin and Mao until he died in office.

With Donald Trump, back in the White House for a second term and eerily imitating Chairman Mao by making his own version of "great disorder under heaven" (大闹天宫) in the United States and elsewhere around the world. With what once had been known as the Free World in such tumult, Xi's charges that democracy was not a superior system of governance—especially as practiced in the United States where ICE (U.S. Immigration and Customs Enforcement) agents were rampaging through American cities arresting immigrants and killing citizens—has suddenly acquired a new and convincing logic. With so many uncertainties, it had become impossible to know just what the U.S. government's posture toward China actually was, never mind how it might evolve. Was it a competitor, an adversary, an enemy, or a deal-making partner? In President Trump's compassless world, it was difficult to predict.

With Donald Trump hurling lightning bolts down on the world like Zeus from Mt. Olympus and even threatening to take a third term like Xi Jinping, Americans were now even uncertain whether their constitutional republic would survive. Those of us who had become used to criticizing China for its rights abuses and autocratic tendencies now found ourselves watching our own country drift toward tyranny. We found ourselves at a confusing and humbling historical moment.

In late March 2026, the Chinese Development Forum convened in Beijing. Before an A-list cast of global CEOs, Chinese Premier Li Qiang proclaimed China to be "a cornerstone of certainty" and "a harbor of stability" that would "work with all parties to promote the optimized and balanced developmetn of trade." But neither China's declarations of stability nor America's fall into its own unique brand of political chaos altered the reality that China's strong tradition of dynastic authoritarianism had under Xi become fused with Leninist principles and modern surveillance technologies to produce a new form of techno-autocracy that truly did represent "a higher stage of Communism." And Xi's impulse to control what was said about China under his rule was no longer a purely domestic matter. When it came to making sure that people "told the China story better" (讲好中国的故事), how it was told abroad was now part of a newly reinvigorated United Front Work Department (统战部) mandate. What was said about China and Xi Jinping in the foreign media was now as important to the Party as what was said inside China.

On one occasion, after I had a long review essay of a book about Xi Jinping's father published in 2026 in *Foreign Affairs*, I got a glimpse of how the increasingly long reach of Beijing's aggressive influence-seeking system in the United States works. The PRC consulate in New York City brazenly called up the editor of *Foreign Affairs*, Daniel Kurtz-Phelan, and demanded a face-to-face meeting. A consular official then appeared at the Council on Foreign Relations to berate him in person for deigning to publish such a revelatory essay.

Even as China seemed to be heading back to the future in ways that were hauntingly totalitarian, it was important not to forget that its society also possessed deep subterranean aquifers of liberal democratic and deeply cosmopolitan thinking that had been quietly pooling up over the past century and had periodically and unexpectedly erupted like geysers to remind us of their seemingly invisible existence. There was the spontaneous gusher of protesters who seemed to come from nowhere in 1976 after the death of Zhou Enlai to flood Tiananmen Square with protest against Mao's brutal and erratic policies; Democracy Wall in 1978, when an unprepossessing brick wall around a public bus yard became a center of overt political dissent for several months; the massive Tiananmen Square demonstrations for democracy in 1989; the outspoken voices like those of the essayist Wei Jingsheng, the astrophysicist Fang Lizhi, and the Nobel Peace laureate Liu Xiaobo. Then there were the more recent expressions of anti-authoritarian sentiment such as the "white paper movement" that erupted against Xi's COVID lockdown in November 2022. And there were myriad other, sometimes quite comical, critiques of Xi Jinping such as the online allusions to him looking like Winnie the Pooh or plump as a dumpling (包子).

Then there was the incident one night in September 2025 when, just as Xi was basking in the glory of his massive military parade in Tiananmen Square, several electronically projected slogans appeared on the side of a high-rise building in Chongqing proclaiming: "Only without the Communist Party can there be a new China" and "No more lies, we want the truth. No more slavery, we want freedom."

The perpetrator of this clever protest turned out to be Qi Hong, a freethinking man who had aimed a powerful projector out a hotel room window that he could operate remotely even after fleeing from China to Britain with his family. This stinging public rebuke of Xi and the Party, which received millions of hits online, served as a poignant reminder of the deep, if suppressed, wellsprings of democratic sentiment that lay beneath the seemingly calm surface of Chinese life, just waiting to find expression.

One other precious democratic inheritance to which the Chinese people held title was Taiwan's democracy. Defying many years of naysaying rationalizations that the Chinese people were "unready" for representative government, the Republic of China on Taiwan managed to bring forth a vibrant, if often tumultuous, democratic government.

So, it is important to remember that whatever the script for the PRC's next act turns out to be, its current autocratic political system, with its codependence on a vast system of prisons for political dissidents, represents one only piece of a far more complex puzzle. The paradox is that now, when China has at last freed itself from foreign domination and has economically regenerated itself in such an impressive manner, Party leaders in Beijing are still depriving their people of openness, justice, freedom, and liberty, the very attributes of civilization that would complete their country's "rejuvenation" and make it an even more triumphant success story than it already is.

This piece of manifestly unfinished business raises a question I had been asking myself for decades: Could piecemeal change ever successfully transform the overall political structure of the People's Republic of China, especially when it came to institutions like its prisons, its reform-through-labor systems, its censorship of the press, and its repressive propaganda apparatus?

The process of editing this manuscript helped me conclude that it was unlikely. Since Stalin bequeathed the idea of a nationwide gulag to Mao, it had become such an integral part of the way China's one-party state worked that it was hard to imagine how it could ever be truly extirpated, short of a far more profound change that would put the whole system at risk.

The Russia scholar and Stalin biographer Stephen Kotkin believes that the fixation on control and rigidity that characterizes Leninist regimes inevitably leads to a level of wariness about upsetting the status quo that makes fundamental change by means of piecemeal reform a virtual impossibility. For as soon as a Leninist regime is pushed near the precipice of real political change, its one-party state *apparat* almost autonomically reacts to arrest the process. This, says Kotkin, was the lesson Chinese leaders took away from Gorbachev's attempts to bring "*glasnost* and *perestoika*, opening and reform," to Russia. Ultimately these reforms, which began in 1985, not only failed, but ended up producing a Vladimir Putin.

When the Soviet Union collapsed in 1991, leaders in Beijing, including Xi Jinping, were paying close attention. The message they received was loud and clear: If they allowed their own reform movement to continue, and if criticism of Mao, like criticism of Stalin by the likes of Nikita Khrushchev, went on unchecked, China would suffer the same fate as the USSR: Its state would erode, its empire be dismembered, and its great power status ended.

"No one had the balls to stand and fight for it [the Soviet Union] when it was being dissolved," Xi claimed in a speech given while touring Guangdong Province in December 2013 that was never officially published. "Why was the Soviet Union dissolved?" he went on to ask. "Why did the

Communist Party of the Soviet Union (CPSU) collapse? One important reason was the struggle in the ideological field. Historical nihilism rejected Soviet Union history, CPSU history, Lenin, and Stalin; it messed up the thinking. As a result, party branches perished; the party could not even control the military. Therefore, a big party like the CPSU was dissipated and a big socialist power like the Soviet Union collapsed. This is a vital historical lesson."

Rather than risk allowing the PRC to suffer the same fate as the USSR, upon taking office Xi set about fortifying China's own Leninist party structures, launching a mass purge against corruption, political challengers, and heterodox ideas that has yet to abate.

Another key part of Xi's playbook to prevent a Soviet-style collapse was to reemphasize the importance of "reunifying the Chinese Motherland" (祖国统一). His model for what constituted the "motherland" was not the modest Ming Dynasty (1368–1644) that was largely limited in geographical scope to Central China, but the far more expansive and grandiose Qing Dynasty (1644–1911) that also embraced the immense territories peripheral to Central China, including Xinjiang, Tibet, Mongolia, Manchuria, Taiwan, Hong Kong, and even the South China Sea.

By the time Xi took office in 2012, there were only three pieces of that larger empire still not fully restored: Hong Kong, Taiwan, and the South China Sea. Our *60 Minutes* investigation happened six years before London handed Hong Kong back to Beijing. The British agreed to do so on the basis of a bilateral agreement negotiated between Margaret Thatcher and Deng Xiaoping that promised the ex-colony that its people would maintain their existing law-based system and "a high degree of autonomy," including free speech, freedom of the press, and rule by law, for the next fifty years.

Despite those promises of "one country two systems" (一国两制), Wu ended his last book with this prophetic warning: "Beijing won't allow Hong Kong to be special, because then it would have 3.2 billion people moving to Hong Kong, this little dot on the edge of China." Instead, he said, it was "inevitable" that China would not only crack down on Hong Kong but try to get Taiwan, too, because the Chinese Communist Party "cannot tolerate a thriving democracy run by Chinese people directly across the water from them." Wu's dictum, delivered before the actual handover of Hong Kong to the PRC, has ended up being ominously prescient.

The Chinese artist Ai Weiwei, who spent most of the first two decades of his life living in a Xinjiang Province *bingtuan* (兵团) labor camp with his "rightist" father, the renowned twentieth-century poet Ai Qing, was equally skeptical of Western hopes that Deng's reform movement would, or could, ever transform his country's political system.

"The West has been wrong about China," he warned. "It was long assumed that capitalism, the emergence of a middle class and the internet would cause China to eventually adopt Western political ideas. But these ideas cannot even begin to take root because the Communist Party has never allowed the intellectual soil needed for them to germinate. And, it never will."

Xi Jinping's determination to make China not just a more centralized and disciplined autocracy but a global power that no other nation—not even the United States—could afford to overlook was perfectly exemplified by his September 2025 military parade in Beijing to mark Japan's defeat in 1945. For this grand spectacle, Xi stood flanked by Russia's Vladimir Putin and North Korea's Kim Jong Un atop Tiananmen Gate to review a procession of impressive Chinese military power that included forty-five phalanxes of marching PLA troops, the latest hypersonic and supersonic missiles, columns of tanks, and floats of drones, as formations of fighter jets streaked overhead.

"The great rejuvenation of China is unstoppable," declared Xi, promising that China's new "world class military" could be counted on to "resolutely safeguard the national sovereignty, unity and territorial integrity of all of the country." Then, sounding almost American, Xi proclaimed, "The Chinese people firmly stand on the right side of history and on the side of human civilization and progress."

It was a calculated display of Chinese military might and Party cant that perfectly symbolized the way the world was dividing, hauntingly reminiscent of the geopolitical bifurcation between Allied and Axis powers during World War II.

"Please give my warmest regards to Vladimir Putin and Kim Jong Un as you conspire against the United States of America," President Donald Trump wrote to Xi on Truth Social, perhaps feeling piqued at not having been invited to join this unholy trinity of top-tier tyrants.

While many Americans had not expected U.S.-China relations to plummet to such depths of enmity, I was not surprised. Having long since acquired an abiding awareness of the fundamentally contradictory nature of the two political systems that underlay the U.S.-PRC divide, what would have surprised me would have been a more friendly convergence. Why? Because there was an insoluble contradiction implicit in conceptions of the two nations' political systems that made the relationship equation impossible to factor. Perhaps Donald Trump's natural proclivities toward autocracy would coalesce at some summit to temporarily smooth the way with Xi Jinping and China. However, it seemed unlikely as I finished final edits on this book that in the long run the deeply rooted and fundamentally republican nature of American society would be changed even by Donald Trump's reign of iconoclasm. The contradiction between these two political systems was too extreme.

Mao himself wrote voluminously on the theory of "contradictions" (矛盾). In his 1937 essay "On Contradiction," he declared that there were two kinds. The first were "contradictions among the people" (人民内部矛盾), where differences between the two opposing sides could be resolved through discussion and negotiation. The second kind were what Mao called "antagonistic contradictions" (敌我矛盾), where the interests of the two opposing sides were so fundamentally incompatible that resolution could come about only through struggle and violence, with one side ultimately triumphing completely over the other. Mao deemed the contradiction between capitalism and socialism and between the United States and China as being in this second category.

As if to remove any remaining doubt about the correctness of the CCP's current policies, just after his epic military parade in 2025, Xi Jinping flew all the way out to Xinjiang for a two-day sojourn. At Urumqi Tianshan International Airport he was greeted by the usual troupes of smiling, dancing, singing minorities. However, this trip was dedicated not to cultural niceties but to reaffirming that he and the Party remained unambiguously committed to existing policies toward Uyghur Muslims.

"Every effort must be made to maintain overall social stability in Xinjiang," CCTV reported him as saying. "It is essential to focus on strengthening grassroots level work, consolidating the foundations and reenforcing the fundamentals to build a people's line of defense against terrorism and for maintaining stability." Then he emphasized, "We must forge a strong sense of community for the Chinese nation as a community, promote the Sinicization of religion in China, strengthen the 'cultural nourishment' of Xinjiang and focus on 'civilizing people through culture.' "

Xi was not relenting on his previous hard lines, either at home or abroad. And the fact that by 2025 Donald Trump had become as retaliatory as Xi in his trade and tariff policies did not bode well for a meaningful and pacific reformulation of the U.S.-China relationship. The contradictions were too deep. So, few were surprised when in April 2025 Chinese Foreign Ministry spokesperson Mao Ning declared, "We are

Chinese. We are not afraid of provocations. We don't back down." Then both social media and state media reprised a black-and-white film clip of Chairman Mao warning the United States during the Korean War in 1953.

"No matter how long this war is going to last, we will never yield," he thundered in his peasant Hunan dialect. "We'll fight until we completely triumph!"

The message was obvious.

Observers were forgiven for wondering where Xi's and Trump's leadership were taking their respective countries. Whether there was any possible way to arrest the dangerous tit-for-tat retaliatory spiral in which U.S.-China relations seemed to have become mired was the question of the hour.

As a summit meeting between Trump and Xi was delayed until May 2026, some observers continued to entertain hopes that the growing disorder in the world would make these two leaders want to reach for some kind of new stabilization of the U.S.-China relationship. Everyone yearened for another 1972 moment when Richard Nixon and Henry Kissinger met with Mao Zedong and Zhou Enlai in Beijing, counterinteruitively setting the two nations on a new course.

POSTSCRIPT

THE POSTPONED XI-TRUMP SUMMIT was back on track, set to begin on May 13, 2026. There was always nostalgia in Beijing for the kind of deeper reset of relations that negotiations between Nixon and Mao brought about in 1972, and some official Chinese media outlets spoke of finding a new "orientation or positioning" (定位) of the US-China relationship. Others had more modest hopes—that these leaders might, at least, be able agree on a new set of guardrails to help guide trade and perhaps even prevent accidental military clashes.

But China's ongoing efforts to manipulate the narrative about its leadership both at home and abroad soon ramped up in a way that became very personal. Once again, I became caught up in the party's efforts to "tell the China story better" (讲好中国的故事). It sought to control what was said about China's progress in a way that evidences many of the concerns expressed in the prior pages.

Having been asked by Daniel Kurtz-Phelan, the editor of *Foreign Affairs*, to cover the summit for his magazine, I prepared to join the presidential trip as a correspondent. This was nothing new to me. I had been part of previous presidential trips to China, including Trump's first visit in 2017, and I was soon duly registered at the White House Press Office. Two weeks later, I was asked to drop my passports off at the White House for submission to the Chinese embassy for a visa. All looked good! On previous presidential trips, it was assumed that the Chinese government accepted that foreign heads of state could bring whatever members of their press corps they wished and would issue a visa to anyone whose name was on the White House's list.

As I waited for news on the next steps, US Secretary of the Treasury Scott Bessent, whom Trump had deputized to plan this trip, called to ask if we could meet in my New York office to discuss summit goals. Intrigued, I agreed. After all, this was the first visit to China by an American president in a decade. In fact, Donald Trump himself made the last trip in 2017.

When two and a half weeks passed without furthSer communications from the White House, I began to worry. My online White House file simply said, "Visa applications are 'under review' at the PRC embassy."

Then, came a terse message from the White House:

To: DL WHO TRAVEL OFFICE
Subject: VISA UPDATE | President Donald J. Trump's
Visit to Beijing, China

> Good morning,
>
> After further guidance from the Embassy of the Republic of China, your visa submission has been *denied.*
>
> Please pick up your dropped off documentation from the White House Lower Press Office at your convenience.

Never mind that the White House referred to the People's Republic of China as the "Republic of China," more commonly known as Taiwan. Far more disturbing was the word "denied" in red font.

Taken aback, I contacted Ivan Kanapathy, a China specialist I knew who was still on a much pared-down White House National Security Council staff. He promised to "reach out" to the Chinese embassy. Two days later, he told me that embassy officials were unmovable, referring to my application as a "policy issue." He also said: "They will not put their refusal into writing."

I was, of course, familiar with such rebukes. But what made this visa denial especially difficult to accept were the implications. If China's punitive response was left unchallenged, the American presidency itself would essentially be put in an embarrassing position. A foreign government dictating whom the US president could include from his country's press corps on his state visit would open the president to charges of being subservient to an authoritarian government.

I had to respond.

From: Orville Schell
To: Kanapathy, Ivan J. EOP/NSC
Subject: Re: Schell Visa for Beijing Summit Denied by PRC
Sent: Wednesday, May 6, 2026 4:33:30 PM

Ivan:

Well, this is a first: The CCP gets to determine who goes on a US President's trip!

Having been on previous presidential trips, I could not have ever imagined it would come to this. Have we become that toothless?

While I appreciate your efforts, I am quite appalled by the outcome.

Regards, Orville

After flying from my New York office to my home in California, I set about undoing all of my preparations. Canceling my plane tickets. Undoing my hotel reservations. Notifying friends and colleagues that I would not be going to Beijing after all. Once again, I'd been tripped up by visa issues. Of course, I was disappointed. I was eager to see Trump and Xi in action again, to write for *Foreign Affairs*, and to visit my wife's elderly parents in Beijing one more time before they died. And, because it was highly unlikely the Chinese government would risk detaining me or preventing me from leaving under such circumstances, I knew that the only way I could dare to return to China was as part of a presidential trip. Furthermore, I understood that as soon as this book was published that it would be impossible for me for me to ever go back. So this latest rebuke left me with a bad taste in my mouth—both about China's habitually punitive behavior and my own country's evident lack of support for a free, open press.

What is more, I was also painfully aware that this unceremonious defenestration from the upcoming summit trip was likely my final excommunication from a country that had for so long been near the center of my life. Now, not only would I miss witnessing the *grande spectacle* of Donald J. Trump and Xi Jinping doing their strange pas de deux, but also I would miss seeing my ailing parents-in-law who had lived with us and helped raise our children in the United States for almost thirty years.

Then . . . something unexpected happened.

While attending a chamber music concert at a friend's house on Sunday, May 11, my phone began to buzz with incoming emails. A discreet check showed they were from the White House.

> Dear Sir/Madam,
>
> This letter is to acknowledge that Orville Schell will be entering the People's Republic of China in an official capacity, serving as a member of the United States Media Delegation in support of President Donald J. Trump's upcoming visit.

Thank you very much for your assistance in this matter.

Sincerely,
Thomas Thorgersen
Special Assistant to the President
Director, The White House Travel Office

Flummoxed, I pinged Ivan Kanapathy.

Ivan:

A confusing missive from the White House.

I assume that I am still considered an apostate.

Orville

He immediately responded.

I think we handled this. We applied some very high-level pressure.

Ivan

More confused than ever, I emailed back.

Ivan:

You note that you "handled this . . . with some very high-level pressure."

> But I have been informed by the White House that the PRC embassy has denied my China visa for this presidential trip.
>
> Am I incorrect?

Ivan replied:

> Beijing has reversed their decision. You should get your visa after all.
>
> That's what they've told me.

Still not quite able to believe what seemed to be happening, I fired off two successive emails to Ivan, trying to work out how I would be able to get my passport back from the White House in time to travel to China. The trip was scheduled for May 14 and 15, just two days away.

Not long thereafter, Victoria Thomas at the US State Department (whom I knew when she had been working with Ambassador Nicholas Burns during the Biden administration) connected me with someone at the Chinese embassy who might help me obtain my actual visa. The embassy staff evidently wanted to have a little "chat," but nevertheless promised same-day delivery of the visa.

"Thank you for whatever magic you worked," I wrote to Ivan. "I know how difficult this all has been."

"See you in China!" he sent back.

To say that that I was gobsmacked by this turn of events would be an understatement. Having been resigned to being unable to return to China, I now had to immediately fly from San Francisco to Washington, somehow retrieve my passport from the White House, rush it to the Chiinese embassy for visa processing at the consular section, dash back to Dulles International Airport for a flight to San Francisco, go home, pack a bag, and then speed back to the airport again for a flight to Beijing.

Somehow, I made it through it all. In the end, I did get to cover Trump and Xi's summit. Just like three decades ago, an unexpected miracle happened at the very last moment, allowing me entrance to China.

Once back in Beijing, I was reminded daily that, besides visa bans, there were now myriad new channels between the United States and China that were also becoming "choke points" (釜底抽薪). Unlike three decades ago, supply chains in trade, business, finance, microchips, pharmaceuticals, solar and battery technologies, critical minerals, rare earths, and many other areas were now being weaponized as mechanisms through which political pressure could be exerted.

As I watched the summit unfold, the dynamic between Trump and Xi was, indeed, bizarre but fascinating. Xi tried to impress Trump with pomp, ceremony, ritual, and access to the secretive Zhongnanhai residential compound near the Forbidden City where China's highest leaders lived in luxurious sequestration. For his part, Trump tried to beguile Xi with unctuous flattery and fatuous praise. But none of these atmospherics succeeded in changing the terms of the game.

It was clear that the issues dividing the People's Republic of China and the United States of America were too numerous to be cut by demonstrations of even the most extravagant expressions of synthetic bonhomie. The divide had become too wide and adversarial to be transcended by these two smiling leaders declaring airy aspirations about finding a way forward via some newly confected vision. In fact, Xi did try to mint just such a vision cum slogan by proclaiming a new era of "constructive strategic stability" (中美建设性战略稳定关系). However, this lofty aspiration only belied the many unresolvable contradictions on which neither side was ready to make any kind of meaningful compromise.

When I arrived at Beijing's Capital Airport to return home, I saw, on a distant tarmac, a strange aircraft that looked nothing like the familiar Boeing and Airbus planes. This one had massive drooping wings and a strangely finned tail. It turned out to be a Russian Ilyushin cargo plane, paving the way for Russian President Vladimir Putin's arrival for his own "summit" with Xi, his twenty-fifth visit. Of course, Xi had already bestowed a special honor on Putin when he invited the latter to stand beside him and North Korean dictator Kim Jong Un as they reviewed a military parade to mark the defeat of Japan in World War II.

Whatever the evolving nature of Xi's "friendship" with Trump ended up being as a result of their summit, it would now be eclipsed by the arrival of Putin, who had previously described Sino-Russian relations as having "no limits." And now here he was again, touting Moscow's relations with Beijing as "already at an unprecedently high level."

So, with Trump's trip had hardly ended, Putin arrived to be feted in the Great Hall of the People, the stolid, Soviet-inspired colossus built during the heyday of Sino-Soviet "friendship" in the 1950s. And once in Beijing, Putin lost no time in proclaiming Russia's new fraternity with China by crowing that both sides were ready to "support each other on issues affecting the core interests of the two countries, including the protection of sovereignty and national unity." "The relationship has continuously deepened and reached the highest level in the new era, a comprehensive strategic partnership of coordination, setting an example for a new type of major-country relationship," he said. And Chinese state media trumpeted the Putin visit as another sign of China's stable standing in a fragmenting world.

Putin's arrival so soon after Trump's departure made the US president's pilgrimage to Beijing look just one of a long series of needy supplicants hurrying to pay tribute to China's latter-day emperor in hopes of winning some promise of support. It was also a reminder for those paying attention that bromides about how "mutual respect and understanding" (相互尊重和理解) between the United States and China might lead to a new era of "constructive strategic stability" (中美建设性战略稳定关系) did not mean that Xi would abandon his alliances with other tyrants like Russia's Vladimir Putin, Belarus's Alexsandr Lukashenko, North Korea's Kim Jong Un, or Iran's mullahs.

During our *60 Minutes* investigation in 1991, we learned that despite all of China's reforms and eagerness to do business with the outside world, there were still many points of deep disagreement between the United States and China that grew out of our very different political systems. These differences would not easily be waved away by a summit meeting. In fact, convergence was even more unlikely in 2026 than in the 1990s. China was, comparatively speaking, far more open in the 1990s compared to the 2020s. Furthermore, when a leader like Xi—who believes "the party's interests comes first" (党的利益在第一位)—is thrown together with an erratic counterpart like Trump, who views diplomatic summits like glorified real estate negotiations, there are bound to be many misalignments.

Many in the Trump Administration seem to hope that the 2026 Beijing summit will echo the 1972 negotiation. But back then, the shared sense of a Soviet threat transformed what had been a hostile Cold War relationship into a more workable one. But that alchemic turning point also depended on the astute negotiating skills of Zhou Enlai and Henry Kissinger. This summit between Xi and Trump possessed no such skilled diplomats and produced to such magic. The results, of course, were marginal.

I expected this to be the last of the many hundreds of trips I have made to China over the past five decades. As I headed to the airport for my flight back to San Francisco, and my cab cruised down perfectly paved, spotlessly clean, tree-lined streets, I was filled with a wistful sense of the paradox of this country toward which I have feel so much attraction and repulsion over my long assiociation. All around me rose the skyline of China's capital, something unimaginable just half a century ago when I first arrived in 1975. The city was then dilapidated, run down by decades of war, revolution, and political mass movements. Back then, it boasted only a single real high-rise building: the Peking Hotel, which had just been opened. But around me now was an endless frieze of towering glass high-rises, manifestations of the very "wealth and power" (富强) for which Chinese of every political persuasion had so long aspired. By any standard, it was an accomplishment that every nationalist and patriotic Chinese could feel proud.

However, there are still important missing pieces to this success story. Even with Deng Xiaoping's reforms, the economic boom in the late 1990s and early 2000s, and the technological revolution and considerable military advances under Xi, the People's Republic had never managed to fundamentally change its Leninist political structure, Marxist-Leninist-Maoist ideology, or its historical narrative of victimization. It had evolved a government that was disciplined, well organized, and even effective, but it had failed to develop those other humanistic traits that make a society truly civilized. The PRC had not developed a greater appreciation for openness, justice, and tolerance. And when it came to matters of dissent and imprisonment for political crimes, China was still embarrassingly retrograde. These were the missing critical parts of Xi's vaunted "China Dream" (中国梦) that night have made his notion of a "rejuvenation" (复兴) more fulsome. After all, those in China who deign to point out what remains undone are still unfailingly persecuted and oppressed while critical foreign observers like me confront denial of access, making our attraction to China feel like being in love with someone who constantly spurns our affections.

And so, as I left Beijing after yet another struggle over a visa, it was a bittersweet departure. My thoughts turned, once again, to Harry Wu.

"Should the world be afraid of China?" Wu asked in one of his last books. His answer was unequivocally blunt but prescient:

> The implications of an economic giant turning into a military and political giant make a contentious relationship with China almost inevitable. Any leader who ignores the deep-rooted Chinese nationalism, does so at his or her own peril and at his or her nation's peril.

ACKNOWLEDGMENTS

I WANT to acknowledge the tenacity of my colleagues at *60 Minutes*, David Gelber and Doug Hamilton.

I also want to extend my heartfelt appreciation and love to Adam and Arlie Hochschild, Larry Friedlander, Tom Engelhardt, and Deirdre English for all their friendship and the careful reading they have given to this and previous manuscripts of mine over the years.

Next, I want to genuflect to my long-gone father and mother, whose interest in the world and whose inclination to act whenever they became aware of injustices shaped my life in profound ways.

And finally, my deepest tahnks to Peter and Amy Bernstein for shepherding this manuscript to print.

INDEX